THE BIG BOOK OF
MANGA

THE BIG BOOK OF MANGA

BARNES & NOBLE

NEW YORK

Illustrations and text: **Ikari Studio (Daniel Vendrell, Santiago Casas, David López)**
Collaboration from Estudio Joso: **Laura Casulleras, Cristina Sánchez,**
Sandra Cardona, Carlos Morilla, Sergi Brosa, Jaime Castaño
Editor: **Cristian Campos**
Editorial Coordination: **Anja Llorella Oriol**
Art Director: **Emma Termes Parera**
Layout: **Gemma Gabarron Vicente**
Translation: **Antonio Moreno**
Copy editing: **Peter Ridding**

www.maomaopublications.com

ISBN-13: 978-1-4351-0174-6
ISBN-10: 1-4351-0174-X

Printed and bound in China

1 3 5 7 9 10 8 6 4 2

Introduction

INTRODUCTION

These days it's impossible to talk about comics without mentioning Japan. After all, it's been the birthplace for a whole new wave of styles, genres and characters that have revolutionized the comic-strip world.

Welcome to the vast and fantastic world of *manga* the origin of which can be found in *Ukyo-e*, one of the most important artistic movements in Japanese history. *Ukyo-e* is, without a doubt, where *manga's* roots are.

Over time, and thanks to the influence European illustrators had on the Japanese tradition, the first precursors to modern *manga* began appearing in the early 20th century in publications like *Tokyo Puck*.

But it was only after World War II that the leisure industry began to extend itself throughout Japan. Back then, a young medicine student who was a big fan of Walt Disney and Max Fleischer, revolutionized the industry with his first *red book* (a 200-page volume published with very poor printing quality). That book was *New Treasure Island* and its author was the young Osamu Tezuka, whose success paved the way for the development of epic tales in the form of comic book series. Tezuka diversified the genre and extended his idea of a comic strip across the whole nation.

Magazines then solidified in their role as the definitive form for spreading *manga*. Among all the magazines published, the one that stood out the most was the innovative *Manga Shonen* (1947), where Tezuka published his legendary *Astroboy*.

With the country's economic boom, the demand for *manga* began to rise. Kodansha, one of the leading Japanese publishing houses entered the magazine market in 1959 with *Shonen Magazine*, which went from being a monthly to becoming a weekly. After Kodansha other publishers began to follow suit, such as Shueisha and Shogakukan.

This is how the *manga* industry became the country's most important form of audiovisual communication.

In the 80's, *anime* became the medium for introducing *manga* to the whole world. Since the 60's lots of Japanese series were emitted on television channels all over the world. Animated adaptations of the most popular *mangas* were devoured by generations of Western children, nurturing the beginning of what would eventually develop into a resounding success. But it wasn't until the 90's that *manga* begun to take-off internationally with Katsuhiro Otomo's *Akira*. Otomo's success, and its film adaptation, became the latest in a line of phenomenona to win over markets around the world. Others were, for example, *Dragon Ball* by Akira Toriyama, and *Grendizer* (also known as *Goldorak*) by Go Nagai, who also created *Mazinguer Z* and is one of the forefathers of the gigantic robot genre.

Nowadays, *manga's* influence is not only visible in the comic industry but also in animation, videogames, cinema and even fashion.

One of the factors that make *manga* a universal graphic and narrative style is its use of imagery. The story, text, dialogue and action depend on the image, making its reading extremely simple and direct. In fact, it can take just a few seconds to read a page of *manga*. Its graphic style is always flashy, full of impact and intense.

This is the cocktail that makes *manga* the number one superpower in the contemporary comic industry.

BASIC MATERIALS

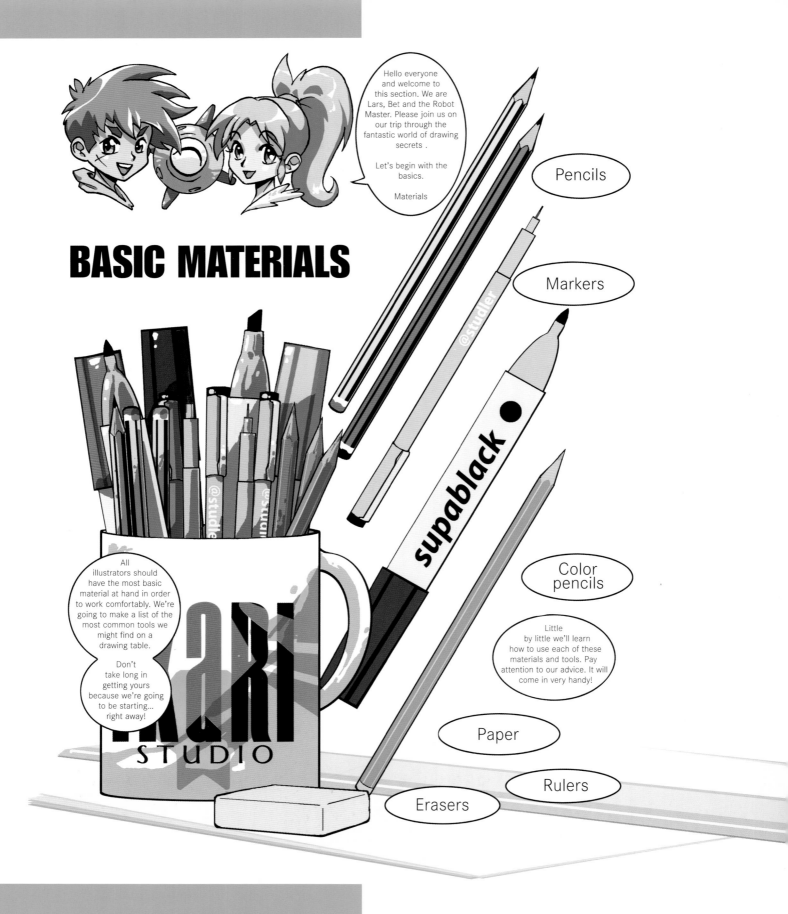

Hello everyone and welcome to this section. We are Lars, Bet and the Robot Master. Please join us on our trip through the fantastic world of drawing secrets.

Let's begin with the basics.

Materials

Pencils

Markers

Color pencils

All illustrators should have the most basic material at hand in order to work comfortably. We're going to make a list of the most common tools we might find on a drawing table.

Don't take long in getting yours because we're going to be starting... right away!

Little by little we'll learn how to use each of these materials and tools. Pay attention to our advice. It will come in very handy!

Paper

Rulers

Erasers

Pencils

Pencils are classified by their hardness. The softer ones, which are called number one pencils, give a greater range of shades of gray and draw darker without applying much pressure. The hardest ones, number three or number four pencils, produce a light gray and you have to press harder on the paper. In the middle we can find number two pencils, which are as good for sketching as they are for drawing details.

Color pencils

Generally used to color illustrations, they are also very useful for sketching. In animation we usually use different colors to mark the different stages of movement, and especially blue pencil since it doesn't mark very much and is very comfortable for sketching. Blue pencil also remains hidden when we use black ink.

Erasers

They are used to correct mistakes, erase pencil marks after working with ink, or to lessen a drawing's intensity. The most common are made of cork. They vary in their hardness, and nowadays ink erasers also exist.

Rulers

These prove to be the best tool for drawing straight lines correctly. We also have curved rulers and templates with different stencils for circles and ovals. All of them will help us draw precise lines.

Paper

Just as with the other materials we've mentioned, we can find a wide variety of drawing paper, and even specific paper for each technique. It's advisable to have a medium quality paper for sketches and a heavier paper for the final drawing. We differentiate paper based on its weight or thickness. In addition, it'll be more or less glossy depending on the amount of cellulose it has.

The ink

Chinese ink is the most common and is ideal for working with fountain pens and paint-brushes. It doesn't dry as quickly as marker ink, but it's more intense and of better quality.

Fountain pens

They are made of metal. We can find calligraphy fountain pens and others that are more specific for drawing, and are of greater or lesser hardness.

Paint-brushes

These are another indispensable tool for illustrators. They're not only used for inking but they're also used for coloring techniques, for correcting, etc. There are many different kinds, made from different materials, each of them especially made and designed for a special technique.

Markers

They are a useful instrument for inking. They make it much easier for us to do precision work with rulers. They are the perfect complement to the paint-brush and fountain pen.

Other tools that can be useful at a given moment are a compass, box cutters, white-out, a drawing table, etc.

Paint-brushes

Ink

LINES AND VOLUMES

The point is the smallest drawing unit. It's the first reference for marking space and has a very strong attraction for the viewer. Try it: if you put one point on a clean sheet of paper your eyes will go straight to it.

Points near each other connect and attract the attention of the reader, who tends to join them together to form concrete shapes.

A line is defined as a succession of infinite points. By its nature, it is usually the basic element of most drawings. It has a lot of values and qualities, such as direction, movement and thickness that make it very expressive.

Straight

Ovals

Circles

Curves

Practice different kinds of lines to create different shapes. It's necessary to train the wrists, hands and arms to have control over them when you begin drawing.

Contours
Lines rarely exist in nature, but we use them to mark limits of objects and changes in tones. That's how we create contours.

There are 3 basic kinds of contours:

The circle, associated with the curve.

The square, associated with a horizontal and a vertical

The triangle, associated with a diagonal.

With the help of perspective and tones we can perfectly represent the three-dimensionality of our world.

Connect two squares with parallel lines and you'll have a cube.

Now, look how we can use flat shapes to draw tridimensional objects.

BASIC VOLUMES

Basic volumes are those with pure shapes. For example, the cube and the sphere. These can be used in drawing to decompose much more complex shapes and make them easier to understand. In other words, we can reduce any complex shape into more basic and simpler volumes that will help us shape and develop our sketch.

These basic volumes are:

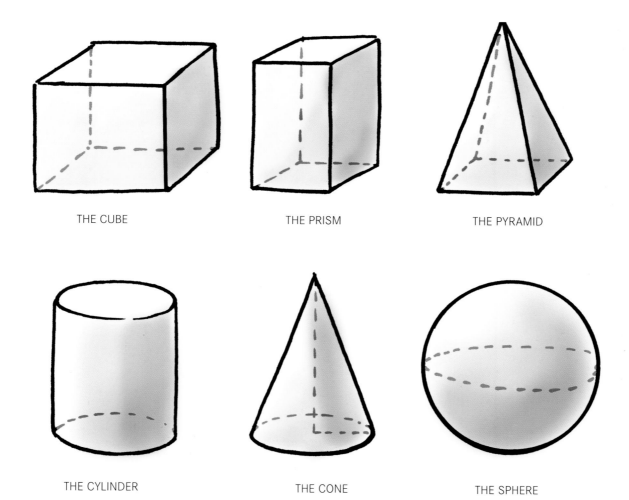

THE CUBE

THE PRISM

THE PYRAMID

THE CYLINDER

THE CONE

THE SPHERE

THE HUMAN MALE BODY

Begin by drawing a long enough vertical line. This will be the drawing's axis of symmetry. We'll draw our character's back over it. The axis of symmetry divides the figure in half. On each side of the axis we find identical elements: eyes, ears, arms, legs, etc.

Next we'll draw an oval at the top of the axis of symmetry: this oval will be the base for our character's head. We'll use head size to divide the axis in eight equal parts. We'll draw an H just above the axis' half-way point: this is where the hips are located.

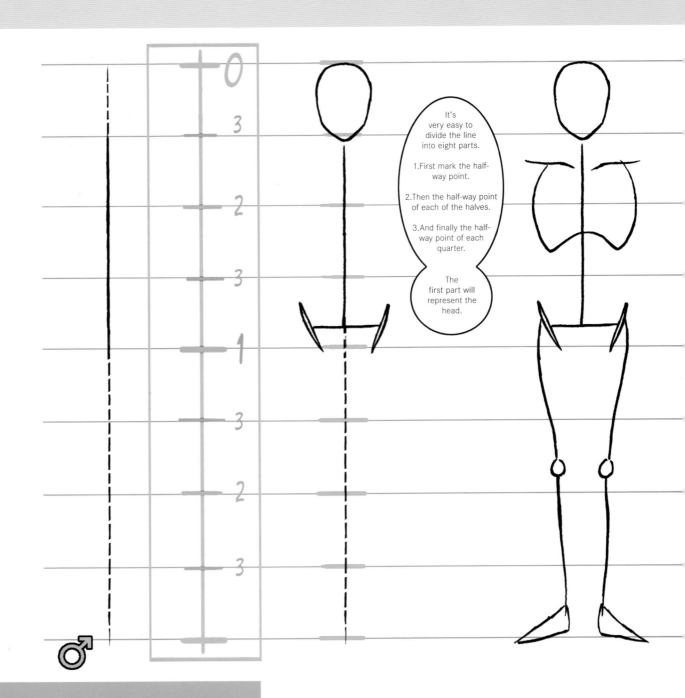

It's very easy to divide the line into eight parts.

1. First mark the half-way point.

2. Then the half-way point of each of the halves.

3. And finally the half-way point of each quarter.

The first part will represent the head.

We'll continue drawing the legs, which will continue up to the last of the eight divisions we've made in the axis of symmetry. We'll differentiate boys and girls when we draw the thoracic box and shoulders. Boys have wider backs, while girls have backs that are slightly smaller or about as wide as their hips.

Finally, we'll draw our figure's arms. The hands extend below the hips. This completes the construction of our mannequin, which will allow us to shape the human body. Shape is the bare-bones skeleton of any drawing. You can't build a house without a foundation.

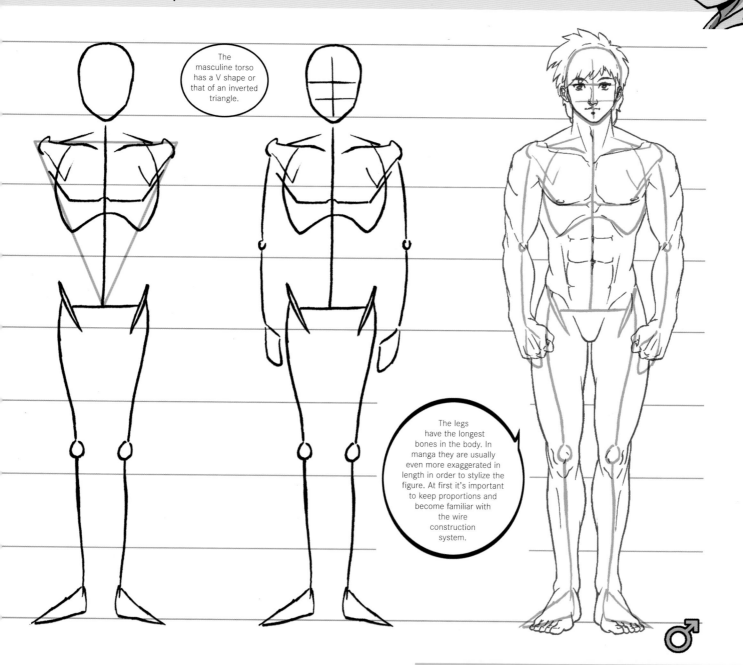

The masculine torso has a V shape or that of an inverted triangle.

The legs have the longest bones in the body. In manga they are usually even more exaggerated in length in order to stylize the figure. At first it's important to keep proportions and become familiar with the wire construction system.

THE HUMAN FEMALE BODY

We'll begin as we did with the male proportions, dividing the space into eight equal parts along the vertical line that will serve our axis of symmetry. If we draw the girl beside a male figure we can use smaller proportions, since they are usually shorter in height. However, it's not always like that, obviously, and it depends on the type of character we are dealing with. Nonetheless, as a general rule, keep in mind that girls are usually shorter than boys.

In the next step we'll draw the differentiating traits of the female structure. The hips are wider than those of boys and their

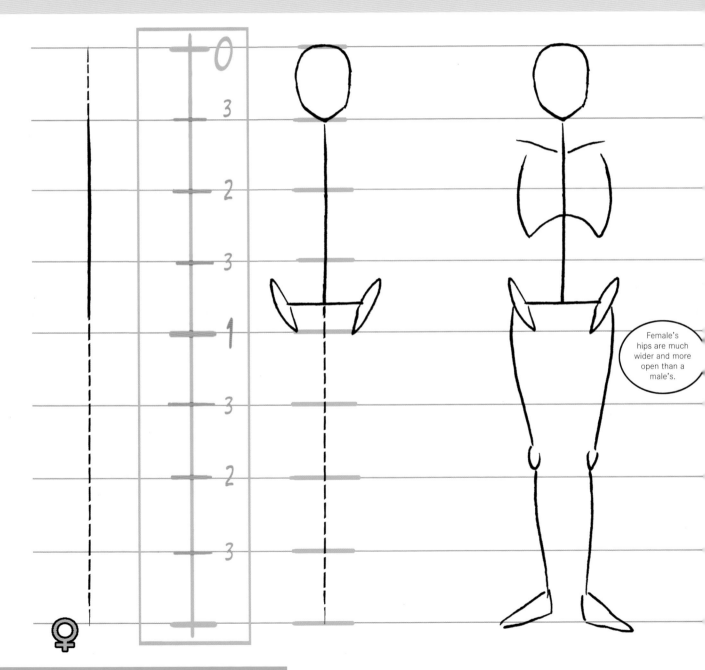

Female's hips are much wider and more open than a male's.

16

shoulders are usually narrower. Their thoracic box is also usually narrower. These differences in shape make their appearance similar to that of an hourglass. There are those who simplify the entire female body with a shape resembling two opposite triangles facing each other at their vertex.

When drawing a woman's shape it's a good idea to use smooth, rounded lines that accentuate the female body.

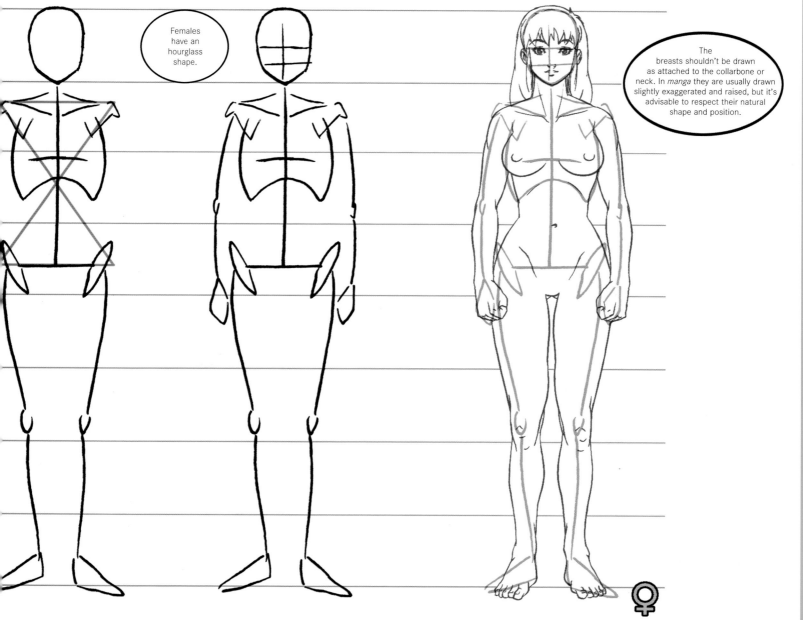

Females have an hourglass shape.

The breasts shouldn't be drawn as attached to the collarbone or neck. In *manga* they are usually drawn slightly exaggerated and raised, but it's advisable to respect their natural shape and position.

SHAPING THE FIGURE

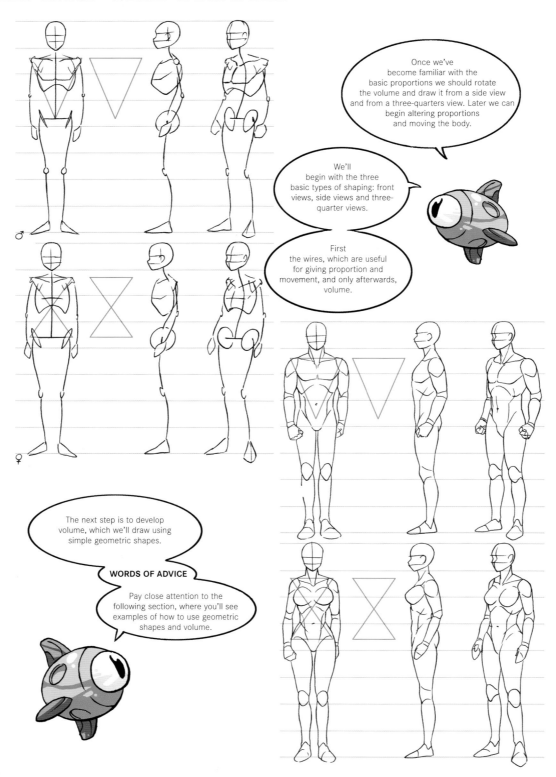

Once we've become familiar with the basic proportions we should rotate the volume and draw it from a side view and from a three-quarters view. Later we can begin altering proportions and moving the body.

We'll begin with the three basic types of shaping: front views, side views and three-quarter views.

First the wires, which are useful for giving proportion and movement, and only afterwards, volume.

The next step is to develop volume, which we'll draw using simple geometric shapes.

WORDS OF ADVICE

Pay close attention to the following section, where you'll see examples of how to use geometric shapes and volume.

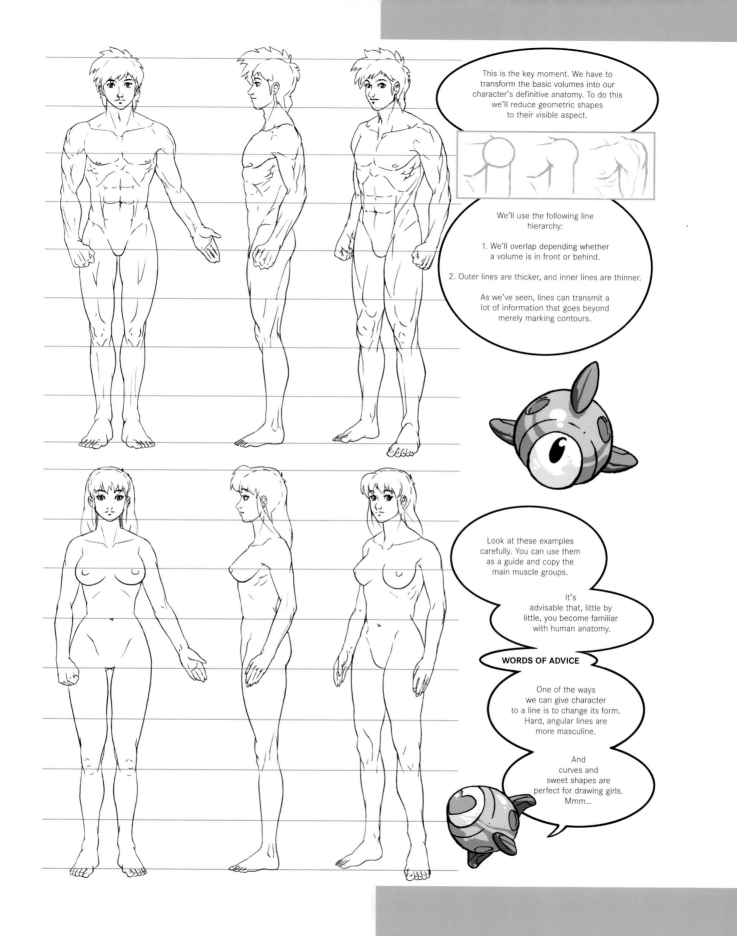

This is the key moment. We have to transform the basic volumes into our character's definitive anatomy. To do this we'll reduce geometric shapes to their visible aspect.

We'll use the following line hierarchy:

1. We'll overlap depending whether a volume is in front or behind.

2. Outer lines are thicker, and inner lines are thinner.

As we've seen, lines can transmit a lot of information that goes beyond merely marking contours.

Look at these examples carefully. You can use them as a guide and copy the main muscle groups.

It's advisable that, little by little, you become familiar with human anatomy.

WORDS OF ADVICE

One of the ways we can give character to a line is to change its form. Hard, angular lines are more masculine.

And curves and sweet shapes are perfect for drawing girls. Mmm...

BODY PARTS

In order to draw different body parts we'll make use of simple geometric shapes and volumes. This can make it much easier to draw complex shapes, such as that of the hands.

In these examples, simple shapes like the circle, triangle or square evolve until they become different points of view of a hand in action.

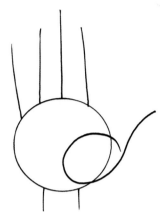

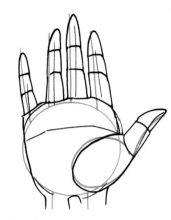

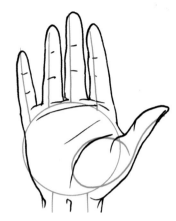

The circumference is associated with a front view of the palm of an open hand. The thumb is always drawn separately because it has its own joint.

When drawing fingers, all of them should fit into just over a quarter of the circumference. The fingers are shaped with small cylinders, with the thumb being slightly larger.

It's good not to draw too many lines in the hands as these will make them look older.

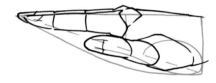

The triangle or half teardrop will help us shape the side-view of the hand.

The greater half of the triangle is for the palm of the hand, and the smaller half for the fingers.

We've sketched and shaped the thumb independently.

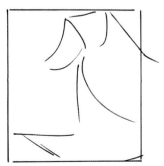

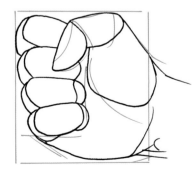

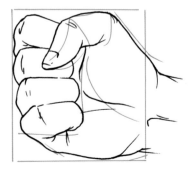

The square is associated with the shape of a clenched fist.

Square or angular geometric shapes transmit rigidity and tension.

In this case the fingers will be foreshortened. We'll use cylinders in order to draw them correctly.

The face, with all its elements, can also be broken down into much simpler shapes that will make it easier for us to give each element its proper proportions.

In the first place we'll draw a vertical line serving as the axis of symmetry, as we did with the complete figures. Next we'll distribute the areas where we'll draw each facial element. We'll mark the line where we'll begin drawing the eyes just below the horizontal axis of the circumference. Below that line, and shortly before reaching the lowest point of the circumference, we'll draw another line which will mark the lower limit of the eyes.Now observe the distance between these two lines (the height of the eyes) which we will call the "eye width". Beginning at the line marking the bottom of the eyes, we'll move down two and a half of the eye widths and draw the chin. We'll mark the nose in the top segment, the mouth in the middle, and the chin in the bottom segment.

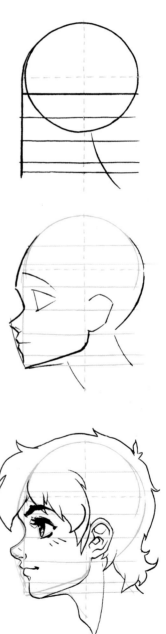

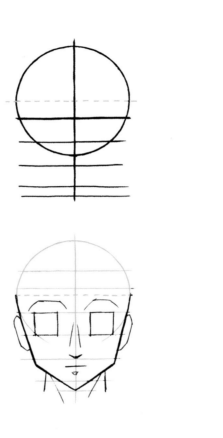

Once we've divided the space, we'll put each element on its corresponding line. The eyes are separated by an eye's distance. And the ears belong at the height of the nose, between the eyes and mouth.
When drawing from a side-view the eyes are much more triangular.

Finally we'll draw each element with great detail, following the way we shaped the volumes and the simple geometric shapes. It's important to give the hair volume and separate it from the line of the cranium. We'll achieve this by using lines conveying movement.

FACIAL EXPRESSION

Facial expressions transmit emotions and moods. When drawing we use facial expressions to emphasize our characters' personality and reveal their inner world. In *manga*, expression is one of the most important areas of a drawing. Especially important are facial expressions, which explore a wide variety of graphic resources and visual metaphors.

Let's learn how to draw the most common expressions by playing with different facial elements.

Basic Expressions

HAPPINESS: Characterized by smiles and wide-open eyes.

SADNESS: We'll curve the ends of the mouth downwards. The facial features fall.

ANGER: A fixed gaze on the subject who has caused the anger. The eyebrows frown and the teeth are clenched.

FEAR: Eyes open and the mouth might open to scream. Generalized shakiness.

DISGUST: The eyes tend to close, the mouth frowns and the nose wrinkles. The head usually turns to avoid looking at whatever it is that is not liked.

INTEREST: Eyes open wider than usual. The head leans towards the object of interest.

Hybrid expressions

Human feelings are much more complex than the six basic expressions we just mentioned. Hybrid expressions stem from the need to faithfully represent the nuances of expression that result when we mix two or more basic expressions.

Let's look at some examples where we combine characteristics from the basic expressions we've already looked at:

INTEREST + HAPPINESS = SURPRISE

HAPPINESS + INTEREST = ADMIRATION

INTEREST + SADNESS = DISBELIEF

SADNESS + INTEREST = BOREDOM

HAPPINESS + ANGER = SADISM

SADNESS + DISGUST = REMORSE

PROPORTIONS

Until now we've only looked at how to shape when dealing with ideal adult proportions, that's to say, a person of perfect proportions. However, we're not always adults, let alone perfect.

ALTHOUGH SOMETIMES I THINK I AM. HA, HA, HA.

When drawing a nine to twelve year old, proportions drop to about six heads in height. At six years old, we use five heads in height. And small children, about four, which is the same proportion we use for an SD (*super-deformed*) character.

SD´s or *super-deformeds* are characters of small proportions with pretty large heads. Our proportions reflect their humorous identity.

After all, proportions say a lot about a character's personality and experience. Now I'm going to show you the main body types and teach you about their characteristics.

The first type we'll look at is the strong build, in which we'll find the athletic type, of ideal proportions; the muscular friend, whose muscles are pure dynamite; the respiratory type, with a large thoracic box.

Let me add a girl to the group, since we can also find real athletic beauties among so many tough guys.

24

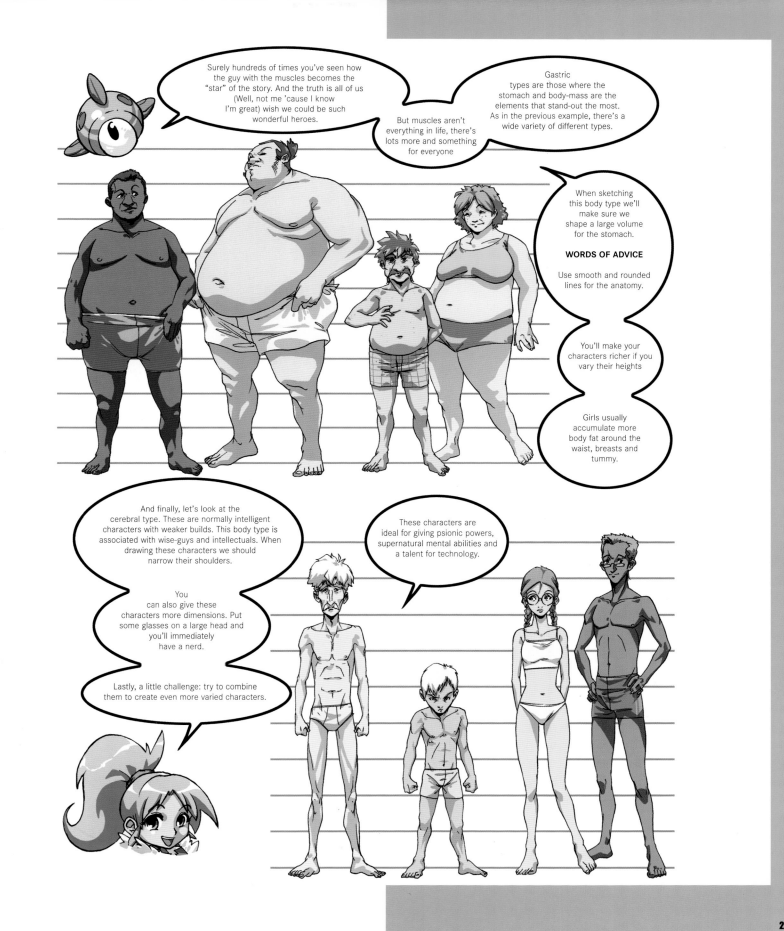

Surely hundreds of times you've seen how the guy with the muscles becomes the "star" of the story. And the truth is all of us (Well, not me 'cause I know I'm great) wish we could be such wonderful heroes.

But muscles aren't everything in life, there's lots more and something for everyone

Gastric types are those where the stomach and body-mass are the elements that stand-out the most. As in the previous example, there's a wide variety of different types.

When sketching this body type we'll make sure we shape a large volume for the stomach.

WORDS OF ADVICE

Use smooth and rounded lines for the anatomy.

You'll make your characters richer if you vary their heights

Girls usually accumulate more body fat around the waist, breasts and tummy.

And finally, let's look at the cerebral type. These are normally intelligent characters with weaker builds. This body type is associated with wise-guys and intellectuals. When drawing these characters we should narrow their shoulders.

These characters are ideal for giving psionic powers, supernatural mental abilities and a talent for technology.

You can also give these characters more dimensions. Put some glasses on a large head and you'll immediately have a nerd.

Lastly, a little challenge: try to combine them to create even more varied characters.

PERSPECTIVE

When we try to draw space, we can use different systems of representation. Perspective is the technique that allows us to represent spatial depth on a flat surface, in addition to being the art of representing objects on a surface the way they look to the eye.

There are different ways of representing depending on the number of vanishing points we use to represent a given point of view.

The horizon is the most important element. We know how objects should be seen just by correctly placing the drawing's horizon. So, if we raise the horizon we'll have a high-angle perspective. But if the horizon is at eye level we'll have an eye-level perspective. Finally, if we lower the horizon to the ground we'll achieve a low-angle perspective.

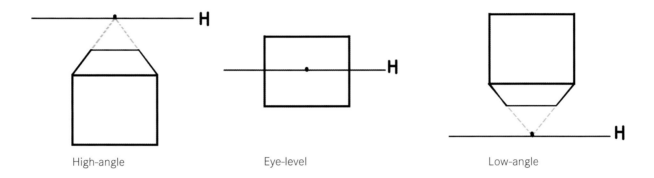

High-angle   Eye-level   Low-angle

Eye level perspective is good for representing objects that are placed parallel to the horizon, and is enough to create simple scenarios. In this case, the vanishing point is placed in the middle of the horizon. We'll look at the cube parallel to one of its sides.

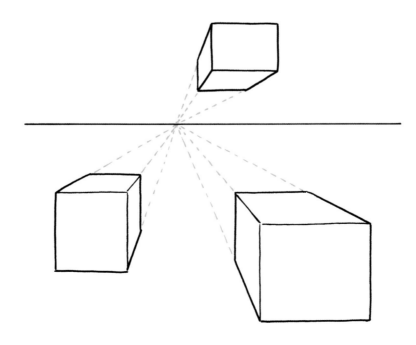

When representing objects that are not parallel to the horizon, in other words, objects placed obliquely in front of the viewer, we'll use a perspective with two vanishing points. In this case we won't position ourselves on a plane parallel to the cube, so there will be one vanishing point for each of the two visible sides. These vanishing points are located outside the field of vision, on the horizon, from left to right.

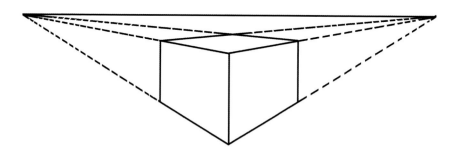

In the case of inclined planes, such as ramps and stairs, we can move the vanishing point along a vertical perpendicular to the horizon in the vanishing points.

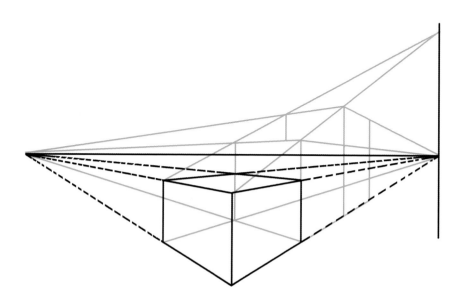

COLOR

Once we've finished drawing an illustration, the next step is to color it. There are lots of ways of coloring and none of them is exclusive to the world of *manga*, although the *anime* look and esthetic, with its flat color techniques, is very typical.

It's a good idea to study a bit of color theory in order to master the relationship between different colors. Color theory is a set of basic rules for mixing and obtaining colors.

There are two basic types of color:

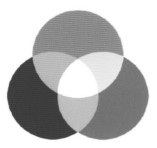

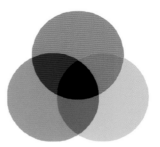

1. Light colors (for example, those we see on a computer screen). These use the primary colors: RGB (red, green and blue). White light is made by mixing these three colors. Partial mixes, or additive synthesis, of these colors create the majority of visible colors in the color spectrum.

2. Pigment colors are those made by subtractive synthesis. These are colors based on the light reflected off pigments applied to surfaces. The base colors are magenta, cyan and yellow. The mix of the three primary pigment colors should produce black, but the color obtained is not intense enough which is why black is added to printing systems, thus creating the color space known as CMYK.

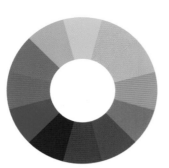

One of the basic aspects of color theory is color harmony.

Harmonic colors are those which produce attractive colors to the sight. The chromatic color wheel is a valuable tool for determining color harmony. Complementary colors are those positioned at opposite ends of the color wheel. Combinations of these colors produce the strongest contrasts.

WORDS OF ADVICE
Before we begin coloring or painting an illustration it's a good idea to carefully finish detailing the lines of the drawing.

When we digitally color an illustration we can use different layers, just as they do in animation. Illustrators who work with animation use different sheets of acetate known as CEL. One of these CELs is used for the drawing, another for the color, and another for the background. When they are superimposed, the different CELs form a single, completely integrated image. We can also use this layer system when using digital coloring programs.

WORDS OF ADVICE: With the drawing "saved" on a separate layer, we can rest assured that we won't destroy it when coloring.

Now the steps to follow are easy:

We'll save one of the CEL sheets for the drawing. The lines on this one should be as clean as possible.

We'll paint each area of the drawing with its flat color.

Here we'll use shading to shape the character and give it volume.

The next step is to adjust lighting, especially on shiny surfaces.

Finally, we can add details, which should always respect the shape of our shadows.

The contrast between the flat color and its shaded tones is greater when coloring shiny objects such as metals.

This is the final result after projecting shadows on the floor.

If we want to draw a background afterwards we can use the same layer system to draw it separately.

GIRLS

SD Girl

High School Girl

Trendy Girl

Idol

Magical Girl

Princess

Fairy

SD Girl

One of the most typical (and most popular) *manga* and *anime* elements is the sailor's outfit or *seera fuku*, as they are called in Japan. Lots of Japanese school girls wear these uniforms, which are also known as *kon* and which usually consist of a blouse with a typical marine collar, a handkerchief tied in front and a pleated skirt that matches the collar. In fact it's not the least bit unusual to see dozens of students dressed up in this uniform out and about on Japanese streets, to the extent that you could say they've actually come to form part of the urban landscape. The student in our composition is wearing this popular outfit, along with a bunch of typical trendy accessories such as her long and loose socks; a little suitcase; a sports bag; hair tied up in a ponytail; and, of course, the ever-present mobile phone with all its little touches. And to finish it off some typical in-between meal snacks.

Shape

The most challenging aspect at this stage is to maintain the correct proportions for a *super-deformed* character. The figure is just about the size of three-heads in height, which creates the effect of a character which is ridiculously small and which looks like a big-headed child. In order to draw the character running and waving, we'll make her pelvis swing and separate her articulations. We'll also tilt her head slightly to give her more personality.

Volume

We'll define the character's volumes using rounded shapes. It's important to maintain the smooth and soft nature of *super-deformed* characters, since it helps them look even more babyish. The use of simple geometric shapes makes it easier for foreshortening areas, such as her right leg which stretches out behind her. We'll move on to shape her face and define the volumes of the character's accessories.

Anatomy

The character's body looks extremely small when you compare it to the size of her head. All the details, such as her fingers and toes, will also keep these comical proportions. We'll move on and define the character's facial features. Her face is very baby-like. She has large eyes, but she also has a tiny nose and mouth, which helps give her that sweet appearance.

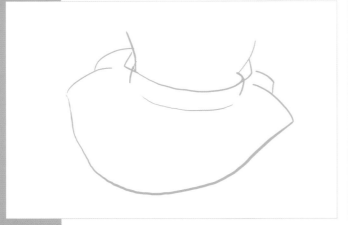

1. To draw her skirt, begin by drawing the volume with simple lines.

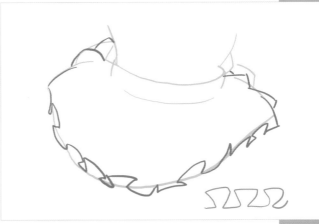

2. Continue by drawing the pleats.

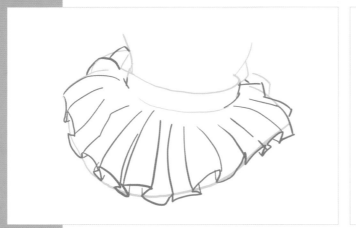

3. Connect the pleats with the waist, giving the lines some volume.

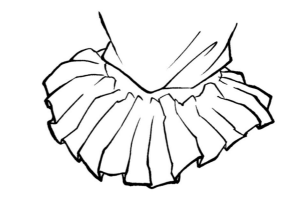

4. Finish by drawing the fabric.

Final Sketch

We've reached the moment for drawing the *seera fuku*. We'll draw the fabric and wrinkles in tune with the tension expressed in the character's gesture. To differentiate the clothes from the girl's flesh we'll use slightly more angular lines. Then we'll proceed with the rest of the elements, such as the cardboard boxes and the mobile phone, which we'll draw with more rigid lines. Her hair clips and pendants help to give her a bit more personality.

Lighting

Studying lighting allows us to develop volume while also lending texture, depending on how much we contrast the tones we've chosen. In this case, the shadows projected by the bag, her hair and skirt will help us separate the different planes of the figure. We'll use smooth, rounded lines to shape the shadows. We must also make sure we use the same criteria for lighting and coloring as we do when drawing the character.

Flat Colors

We'll choose typical colors, blue and white, so as not to get lost in experiments with color. This combination isn't standard but it is pretty common and "safe" from the drawer's perspective, leaving little room for mistakes with using these two colors. The schools that don't dress up in this uniform and opt for a blazer and tie also tend to combine different colors such as brown, green etc.

Shading

We'll pay attention to our lighting reference when using color to shape the character's main volumes. Shadows aren't merely darker colors but are obtained by saturating the tone slightly to create more brightness within the drawing. Since we're using a zenithal light focus, we'll accentuate the shadows the closer we get to the lower areas of the character.

Finishing Touches

It's time to give the drawing its finishing touches. Let's lighten up her skin and hair, which are usually shinier than the other elements (such as the clothes, which are matt). We'll also add highlights to her eyes and the screen of her mobile phone. Then we'll project her shadow in order to define the position of the floor. This way it doesn't look like our character is floating in space. The visual metaphor of the little heart will round out the illustration.

High School Girl

High School teenage girls are without a doubt the biggest stars in the *shojo* genre. This is logical, since they're precisely the ones reading this type of *manga*. However, their leading role isn't just limited to the *shojo* genre. In *manga* in general, female characters play a bigger part than in any other style of comic. This is one of the reasons *manga* has won favor with girls all over the world, bringing them closer to the huge world of story-telling. The high school and collegiate prototype has changed over time, and this type of character has taken great strides, gaining in strength, independence and prominence, following a similar process to women in Japanese society, which traditionally revolves more around men. These adolescent female characters dress up in the typical Japanese schoolgirl uniform and aim to portray the average student, which ultimately allows for more readers to be able to identify with them.

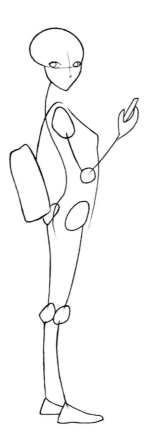

Shape

For this character we're going to be looking for a simple shape that gives us a chance to see her main characteristics at first glance, so we won't need to be making second sketches. We've chosen to play with a side-view of her body and with a three-quarter view of her face in order to quickly see all her fashion accessories, as well as her full facial expression.

Volume

As we saw before, we can draw the basic structure of the figure using simple volumes: cylinders and spheres. Here we can visualize how the different volumes are going to interact, how one depends upon the others. The clearest example of this is her rucksack, and its relation to her shoulders and hips. With this type of pose, it's also very important to mark the twisting of her trunk.

Anatomy

Now is the time to give our figure's body some character. We'll have to think about her anatomy in order to accomplish this. She's an adolescent, but still not a fully-fledged woman, so let's not exaggerate her feminine attributes. This will make her more neutral and closer to "average", so more readers can identify with her. Her hair should always be clearly differentiated from her body, and this can be accomplished using looser lines.

Final Sketch

Designing her costume is crucial here. In this type of character, the uniform is the distinguishing element that identifies the girls with their school, giving them a strong identity. It's a good idea to use different types of lines and wrinkles to treat each item of clothing according to its material and shape. For example, in this case the pleats of her skirt are more angular and geometrical than the wrinkles on her loose socks.

Lighting

In order to correctly define a character, it's best to use natural zenithal lighting, as if it were an outdoor scene bathed in sunlight. In this case we'll see how the shadows gather on the lower parts of objects. Sometimes in *manga* the same line economy that forces one to draw simplified faces also applies when we're drawing shadows, making the faces look fresher and more attractive.

Flat Colors

Here we'll decide on the colors we'll be using for our character's school uniform. Generally we'll choose color combinations that aren't too colorful or exaggerated. If we move away from the typical navy blue, we can opt to combine greenish shades and earthy colors. Don't see it as a limitation, since you have a wide assortment of bright, rich tones at your fingertips.

Shading

As we did in the lighting section, here we'll also mark the volumes of our character. When shading, it's important to use different contours for each surface, and likewise, we must treat each fabric differently. In doing so we're adding yet another differentiating trait to each of the elements in the illustration. The doll hanging from the mobile phone gives a touch of color that lightens up the composition.

1. We've already learned how to draw the skirt. Now we're going to give this one a pattern. First, shape the shadows following each volume.

2. Next, draw the pattern following the creases in the clothes. We can find inspiration for our design in the typical Scottish pattern.

3. Lastly, add shading to the pattern we've just finished drawing, following the same guidelines as her skirt.

Finishing Touches

An easy way of forcing the viewer to focus his attention on the part of the drawing that interests us is by using the circumference, guiding his eye to the center, thus drawing the viewer towards the character's face. We'll use a neutral color so that it doesn't take over the character. In order to maintain tonal coherence, we'll also be choosing a color from the same tonal range as the rest of the composition.

Trendy Girl

Dressing up in the latest fashion, always up to date with the latest trends, dyed hair and extravagant hairstyles, the very latest extreme fashion accessories, these are the *gals*, Japanese girls, students in their majority, who love being in tune with the latest fashion. They have platform shoes, mini-skirts, make-up, handbags, different color dyes for their hair, etc. *Gals* are crazy about fashion and all their time and money is spent on it.

We can identify various types of *gals* depending on their skin color and clothes: *ganjiro* who have white skin; *ganjiro*, who have darker skin; *loko* who boast more extreme colors; and *hime* who look like modern princesses.

For this illustration we'll peek into their intimate selves. We're going to seek out an original focus and try to capture an introspective snapshot of a type of character that revolves almost exclusively around its outward appearance. We'll draw our character as she's looking through a fashion magazine choosing her next acquisitions.

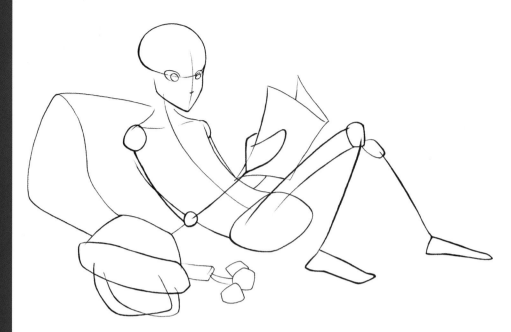

Shape

In order to give shape to a figure that is sitting or lying down, it's best to first draw the resting points and parts of the figure that will bear the brunt of the weight. In this case, the cushion the girl is using as support is her back and her hips. Since it's a relaxed position, the majority of the lines will be soft curves. We'll do away with lines of tension. Drawing the magazine will help us shape her hands.

Volume

The most important thing here is to establish depth in our image. We have to decide which volumes are superimposed on the others and maintain the character's perspective with relation to the floor her hip is resting on. The position of her hands, delicate and subtle, gives us clues about her character. We'll also draw the volumes of her fashion accessories, making sure that each of them hangs naturally, in tune with her relaxed position.

Anatomy

These types of characters pay a lot of attention to their physical appearance. They are usually thin teenage girls with delicate bodies. We'll look to create an expression that reflects our character's interest in the magazine she's reading. This will be the central object and her gaze should be on its pages. Details like a well-kept hairstyle or nails, which are very long, give us more information about our character's interests.

Final Sketch

Despite the intimacy of the scene, clothing is crucial when drawing this character. We'll have to pay great attention when drawing the fashion accessories she's wearing: bracelets, belts, ankle bracelets, hair-clips, etc. The magazine she's holding is definitely a fashion magazine but the suggestion of a title is all you need. Accessories such as her cushion and bag should also reflect this girl's taste for fashion.

Lighting

The shadow projected by the character is another of the elements that we have to keep in mind when defining the space between the character, the floor and the resting points. Shadows should be drawn using soft, rounded lines, without many angles, to give the image a sweeter look about it. Once again, changing colors and contrasting them will help differentiate textures, such as the shiny telephone screen.

Flat Colors

The colors used for the illustration must be appropriate for the character. Pastel pink is usually a *gal* favorite, so we'll go with that with this character. Since this shade of pink tends towards purple, we can combine it with cream colors that tend towards yellow, since these are complementary colors. It's also very important to match the color of her clothes with her fashion accessories.

Shading

The colors chosen for the shadows should belong to the same tonal range as the ones mentioned previously, but without darkening or saturating them. This way we'll be respecting our initial concept by keeping the illustration within a range of soft tones. The idea is to create a subtle, local custom image that is very precise in portraying our character's personality.

1. At the last moment we decided to slightly alter the composition of the drawing from a horizontal format to a triangular one.

2. To do this we've added an element that will help us recover part of the image's upright positioning: a lamp.

3. The lamp fits in with the general style of the drawing. After coloring it and adapting it to the image's perspective, we'll finally place it behind our character.

Finishing Touches

Now the drawing has recovered its vertical aspect. The structure of the composition is more triangular and the magazine, which is the center of our character's attention, and acts as the central axis of the illustration, stands out against the rest of the elements with its yellow color contrasting with the shades of pink around it. In fact, color can play a major role in a composition as we've just seen here.

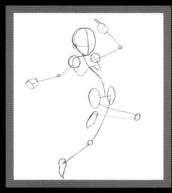

Idol

The *idol* phenomenon began in the early 70's in Japan. Basically, *idols* are girls between the ages of 16 and 21 who are entirely devoted to the pop world. Basically, all Japanese teenage girls need to become an *idol* is an attractive body and a lot of charisma. They should also have an impeccable moral conduct since they also serve as role models for the thousands of fans they will go on to entertain throughout their career. The *idol* phenomenon is a bit like the spotlight that revolves around rock stars and the more famous sports stars in the West. And naturally as we'd expect, we can find hundreds of *manga* series dedicated to the *idol* world, such as *Idol Tenshi Youkoso Yoko*, *Idol Project* and *Lovedol Lovely Idol*, although perhaps the biggest and best example of them all is *Idol Densetsu Eriko*, a series from the late 80's.

Shape

We've chosen a front view which will help us try to capture the girl's movement across the stage as she's singing a song. We'll accentuate this movement by arching her back and taking advantage of this to draw a flexed leg that makes the most of this effect. We'll also get help from the position of her left leg, which looks a little like it's jumping.

Volume

We'll use cylindrical shapes to draw the volume of her hair, which is the element that best defines the character's movement in this illustration. We'll also define the shape of her hands. One of them holds the microphone, while the other grips the microphone stand. We'll mark the position of her feet using simple shapes that make their volume clear.

Anatomy

We'll give her hair and all the other details shape, while also defining the shape of her body. Since she's an *idol* we should draw her with a kind and attractive face. That's why we chose this gesture of glee. She's also winking to the fans that are watching her perform. The position of her left pinky gives the character some charisma since it's a personal gesture.

Final Sketch

We'll add her clothing and final details, such as the bow tie round her neck. The base of the microphone stand will also help to make the image more dynamic. Her attire should fit the character's movements and that's why the dress flows, while the handkerchief on her waist moves in the opposite direction to the girl. We'll take advantage at this stage to smooth the character's lines and hair.

Lighting

In the majority of stages designed for music performances the lighting usually comes from a strip of spotlights that are aligned overhead. Ours is no exception, so we'll be using a zenithal light that will serve to correctly mark the shadows and define texture to perfection.

Flat Colors

The character should transmit happiness and dynamism, so we'll be using bright, attractive, saturated colors that reflect these feelings. The microphone stand will serve as the starting point for the girl's movement, so we'll be painting it in a dark color that contrasts with her, placing them on different dimensional planes.

Shading

We'll begin defining the textures, as we can see with the microphone, and shape the character's volume. We should pay attention to the shadows made by her clothing, in this case the shadow projected by her skirt on her legs. We'll use a color of the same tone, but slightly darker, to draw the pupil of her eye, which will add depth.

Tips and Tricks

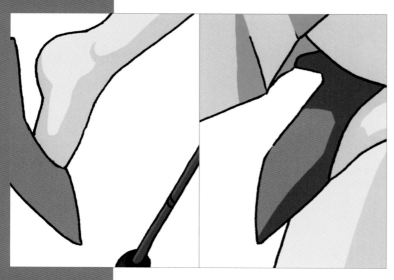

1. We'll color her shoes using a technique that can also be useful when painting different shiny surfaces, such as the hull of a boat or the texture of an airplane. We'll use the shadows we described in the previous steps.

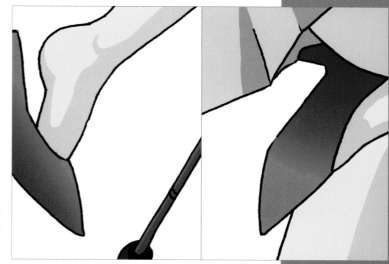

2. On a separate layer we'll create a diminishing range of reds that follows the drawing's light source, while respecting the surface of the shoe.

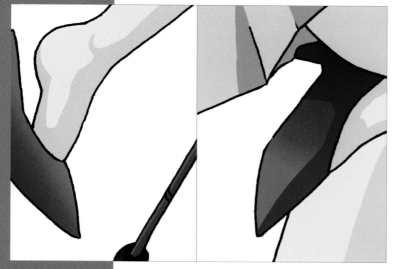

3. Once we've finished this gradation we'll combine it with the shadows we have already added.

Finishing Touches

We'll add some finishing touches, such as the white of her shoes, which makes their surface shinier. We'll give her hair some highlights, paying extra attention to her pigtails, which we'll shape to help us give our character movement. Lastly, we'll add a simple, but effective background using the colors we've used on our character. We should make sure they don't mix so as not to lose depth.

Magical Girl

The genre of *Magical Girls* or *maho shojo* encompasses a world of *manga* and *anime* where the main characters are girls who, thanks to some magical power are suddenly transformed into heroines ready to save the day. Generally speaking, these are stories where the local color of everyday school life intermingles with fantastic adventures taking place in marvelous magical worlds that the characters are dragged off into thanks to their powers. Some examples of famous comics of this genre are *Sailor Moon*, *CardCaptor Sakura* and *Doremi*. The main characteristics distinguishing these types of girls are their connection with some sort of magical object that gives them their special powers and the bombastic outfits they dress up in. Sometimes inspiration can be found in a schoolgirl uniform, or even a wedding dress, that is then transformed and overloaded with colorful fashion accessories, such as tiaras, wings, boots and ribbons.

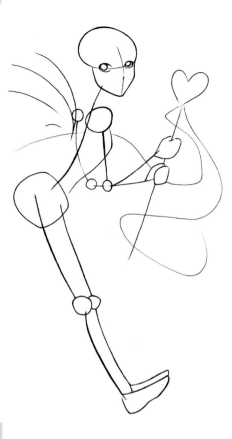

Shape

We'll use a similar layout as the one used in the High School Girl exercise, but this time, we'll try to make it look like our character is floating on air, perhaps with the help of one of her special powers. This is a classic position in *Magical Girl* illustrations. In order to express movement, it's best to curve her back, which will also affect the rest of the figure's position.

Volume

The best way to exaggerate the movement of her back is to also exaggerate the position of her pelvis. Even when we're drawing a relatively static pose it's a good idea to give a character the kind of body-language that makes it come alive. We'll also shape her main accessories: her staff and wings.

Anatomy

As we've already said, the main characters in these comics are usually girls or teenagers, and their anatomy should be reflective of this. We're normally working with stylized characters, sometimes even ones somewhat languid. Other times, the magical transformation process makes our character's body evolve from a girl into an adolescent, but we should never exaggerate her feminine attributes too much.

Final Sketch

We've reached a crucial moment when drawing this type of character: it's time to design her costume. We can find conceptual masterpieces in the designs used in some of the series we mentioned previously. Generally speaking, they use daring combinations of skirts with other clothing items on top that are based on uniforms. We'll add exaggerated fashion accessories and a great many ornamental details that might even verge on the baroque.

Lighting

As we said in the previous section, a good deal of their attraction lies in the complexity of their clothing. Shaping the shadows allows us to exaggerate the volume of her skirt, while her shoulder pads accentuate the movement of her ribbons and the shape of her wings, further exaggerating their splendor. The shadows will also help us separate elements on different planes.

Flat Colors

The colors used when drawing *Magical Girls* are always bright. Different color combinations can be used to connect them to their origin, their abilities, their personality or their powers. Thus color becomes one of the main identifying elements for each of the girls, especially in a serie where the protagonist is not the only *Magical Girl* but is among a group of them.

Shading

At this stage we'll basically be following the same steps as with the lighting. However, shading an illustration is somewhat more complex. This way we can see how to enrich our shaping by applying other colors in our layers of shading, so that we're not merely limiting ourselves to shaping the volumes.

1. Using complementary colors is a typical way to go about shading. We'll achieve softer shadows if we avoid saturating the illustration with dark colors like black.

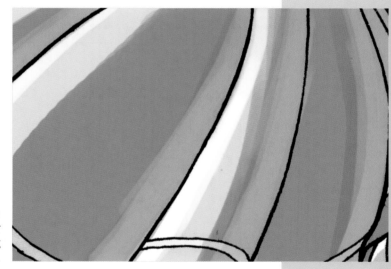

2. We can add effects that reflect light within the shadow itself. This way we'll draw larger shadows and keep the image from looking too flat.

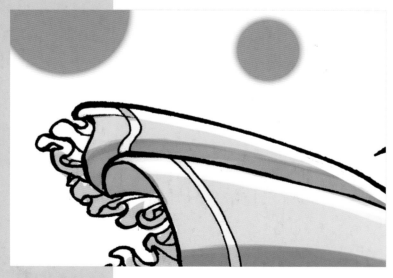

3. A second light focus or perhaps some magical sparkles can serve to reflect color within a shadow.

Finishing Touches

Reflecting light within shaded areas and using complementary colors has helped us create a warm, magical atmosphere around the *Magical Girl*. In this type of character it's important to combine ranges of colors that give off pleasant brightness even when shaded. Effects such as sparkles, highlights, etc. are perfect tools that can be used to enrich these kinds of illustrations.

Princess

Lots of young girls dream of becoming princesses. To a large extent they are the source of greatest admiration in medieval fantasy tales. Anyone who reads these will notice that they represent virtues such as beauty, honor, elegance, goodness, innocence and happiness. If we consider the importance of the feminine role in *manga* stories, we can see it's perfectly understandable that these princesses don't always have to play the subservient part of a damsel in distress, always waiting to be rescued by her chivalrous knight in shining armor. It's relatively easy to find hardened princesses that defend the values they believe in with all their might, generally tied to compassion, justice and freedom. We should take advantage of these characteristics in *manga* and design a beautiful and delicate princess who is majestic and sensual but with a look in her eyes that allows us to imagine the warrior inside her.

Shape

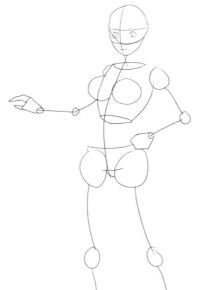

Without a doubt, the three-quarter perspective is ideal when presenting a character for the first time. This perspective works best to give the most information about the subject we are drawing. We can shape our princess by choosing a natural, relaxed position. The gesture she makes with her hand indicates her aristocratic nature.

Volume

When framing a position it's necessary to place the character's feet correctly. It's very probable that we won't see them when we finish drawing her costume, but it's very important to know our character's entire body in order to draw it correctly and maintain its proportions. In the three-quarter position the feet are unaligned, with one of them slightly on top of the other by way of the perspective.

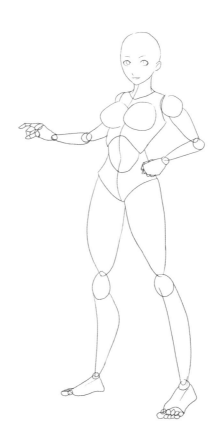

Anatomy

Once again we'll be drawing the body of a young, beautiful girl. The silhouette is usually svelte and stylized, and to draw it correctly we'll use the trick of slightly elongating her legs. This makes her hourglass shape more evident. We can also begin to plan the effect the corset has on the princess' breasts. Her hair blowing free in the wind lends movement to poses that are otherwise rather static.

Final Sketch

The dress is the center of attention in this drawing. Before we allow our imagination to run free it's a good idea to find references when designing costumes for characters like princesses, empresses or any other royal lady. It's always a good idea to look at royal designs in order to have a solid base on which we can develop our most fantastic ideas. A delicate crown reveals this young girl's important rank.

Lighting

In this case lighting will merely shape the character, without creating a special dramatic effect. For her dress, and for whenever we want to show a fine, delicate texture, we'll choose tones that don't darken or contrast too much with our original color. Both her skin and her dress reveal delicate shadows, with the difference being that we'll use more angular lines on the fabrics and gentler lines on her body.

Flat Colors

Once again we'll be using a range of pinks in this illustration. When we color characters like this one, it's best to use pastel colors that are not too saturated and very luminous. Pastel yellows, blues and pinks work best in cases like this. White can also be a good choice, but it's usually reserved for special occasions since it's the color most closely connected with virtue.

Shading

Female characters of this nature usually represent goodness. That's why it's a good idea to use soft, bright colors, even when it comes to shading, and really try to avoid darkening the illustration. The most important part is how we do her costume. It needs to have "body" to give it the appearance of spherical volume.

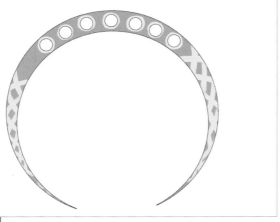

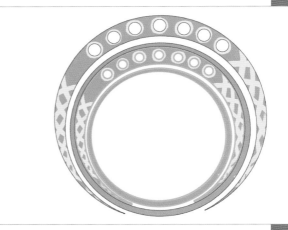

1. So you can't think of a good idea to complement your drawing and give it greater detail? All you have to do is look at art history, a trick used by illustrators all over the world.

2. Modernist and *art nouveau* decorations inspired by natural and purely geometrical shapes can also serve as good inspiration.

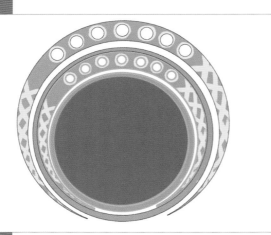

3. In order to draw these kinds of decorative elements, first we must draw their center. Afterwards we'll draw the main circumference area that marks off the work space, and finally we'll finish the rest of the embellishments using a compass and curved stencils.

4. The cloud in the center of the illustration will finish it off, giving us the effect of a "drawing within a drawing".

Finishing Touches

We'll compose the image with the character and the background. At this stage digital coloring facilitates how we blend different elements using color correction systems. These tools allow us to tone the final image so that the different elements don't look independent from one another but integral pieces of the same drawing. For this illustration we've chosen a bright, luminous color tone.

Fairy

Of all the magical creatures we might find in the different mythological fantasy worlds across our planet, fairies are perhaps one of the most important. Or, at the least, we can say they hold a privileged position in the pantheon of fantasy characters. Way back in medieval tales fairies were always connected to the world of spells and enchantments. Initially they were believed to be of human size, but the tiny, ethereal creatures described by Shakespeare in *A Midsummer Night's Dream* influenced subsequent visions of these characters. These small spirits of nature are proud to be regarded as the protectors of the Earth's natural landscapes. Fairies are usually represented as tiny female figures with fairy features. Generally they are depicted with wings, giving them the ability to fly, among other marvelous powers. They are said to be guardians of the forests, rivers and mountains, and so there are dozens of different types of fairies.

Fairies usually look like young girls. Once again, we can practice shaping the female figure. As always, the main differentiating characteristic is their hips, which are wider than those of male characters. By relaxing the positioning of her legs we'll make it look like our figure is floating. Finally, we'll give her some wings.

Volume

At this point in the illustration, the best way of going about giving our female character structure is to use rounded volumes that faithfully represent the shape of a woman's torso, which is similar to a conventional hourglass. These volumes will also help stylize the anatomy of her legs, thus giving her an exuberant contour.

Anatomy

As we've said before, fairies are characterized by their fairy features. These can be, among other things, their pointy ears, almond-shaped eyes, high and well-shaped eyebrows, small noses, etc. When drawing our fairy's face we should keep these characteristics in mind in order to make them evident and give them importance. Otherwise, their bodies are just like any other beautiful, svelte woman.

Final Sketch

The clothes worn by fairies are usually inspired by elements from nature, in their choice of designs as well as in the types of materials used. We can find, for example, designs inspired by the shapes of flowers, with skirts similar to a crown of petals; or dresses made entirely out of flowers, where the stems serve as ribbons and the leaves as the skirt.

Lighting

Fairies are beings of a delicate nature. We should respect this personality trait even when shaping the figure. The shape of the shadows should be soft and rounded, and not consist of any angular shapes. This will prevent us from giving our fairy a rough look. The contrasts should also be delicate and subtle, not at all aggressive.

Flat colors

Colors from the world of nature are always present in the clothes worn by a fairy. The colors of plants and flowers are the ones most commonly used for their outfits. For our fairy we've chosen green, which is the color most closely connected with nature. We've complemented this by using pink tones for the color of her hair and eyes. In manga it's quite common to find unusual or unnatural colors being used when it comes to hairstyles.

Shading

We'll select colors for the shadows in the illustration from among the more saturated tones of the colors we've chosen previously. The final result aims to be an illustration that is magical and colorful, and this is a good way to go about achieving it. We've chosen a soft, transparent tone for her wings. We'll work it like a veil, which is what it will look like in the end.

1. Complete the illustration by drawing little spirits in the forests.

2. These spirits can be strange-looking fires in the shape of butterflies. Add a magical aura that blurs her contours.

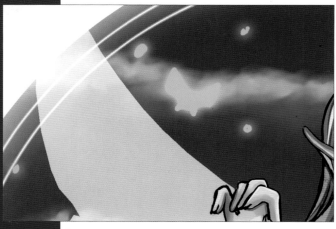

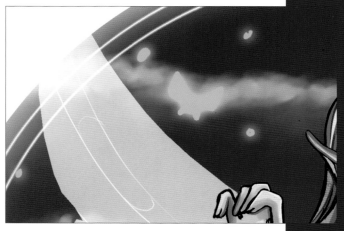

3. For her wings use the same method we spoke about earlier. In the first image we see the wing as transparent with respect to the background.

4. Next, draw the fibrous structure of her wings.

5. Finally, blur the contour lines, giving her that magical aura as mentioned in Step 2.

Finishing Touches

Just like the wide majority of beings in the magic kingdom, fairies usually appear at night, surrounded by a magical halo. That is why we've given the illustration a nocturnal background that highlights this characteristic. Magic powder seems to fall from her wings, helping her float in the air. The highlights on her contour reflect the magical light bathing the scene.

SWEET

Puppy Girl

Candy Girl

Baby Doll

Angel

Puppy Girl

Japan is definitely one of the most fetishist countries in the world. However, we're not just referring to their rich and complex folkloric tradition, but their devotion to the most incredible variety of unimaginable topics. That's how *moe* was born, which can be translated as "budding", or fetishism related to the fields of *manga* and *anime*. Any character from any serial can be considered *moe*, although females are especially susceptible. You could say there is a type of *moe* for every *otaku*, but some are much more popular than others. For example, girls with glasses or *meganekko*, and girls with cat ears or *nekomimi*, have their own specific audiences. On the other hand, a girl that is simply "pretty" by contemporary beauty standards can also be considered *moe*. So what happens when we combine a *kawaii* or "cute" girl with one who is *moe*?

Shape

Let's sketch a young girl who we'll dress up in an adorable, provocative cat outfit. We'll draw her on all fours on the floor, in a feline position. Her spinal column is a pronounced curve from her neck to the end of her tail (the tail is merely an extension of the spinal column). She supports herself with one hand, while the other holds up a mouse that she's just caught.

Volume

Let's mark the girl's volumes, which are especially exaggerated at the hands and feet since she has furry paws. We'll pay extra attention when drawing the curve of her back, particularly where her thoracic box meets her waist. Her spinal column's articulation plays an important part here, and is represented in the drawing with a sphere that also marks the volume of her belly.

Anatomy

Since the figure is wearing little clothing we must take care to develop her anatomy correctly when drawing her contours. Her supporting arm is rigid, while her hand's gesture is delicate. We'll give her a naughty expression, with her eyelids slightly closed and a fixed gaze. Her short, but pronounced, eyebrows and the fang sticking out also help.

Final Sketch

We'll use clothing to give our cat girl some charisma. The furry outfit is made of two parts, an upper and a lower part, with matching paws on her hands and feet, a cat-ear diadem on her head and a cat's tail. We'll draw a discontinuous, sharp-pointed contour that imitates the fuzzy material. The toy mouse she's just caught, which is hanging from her hand, adds a touch of humor.

Lighting

In this case light comes from the upper left part of the illustration. It's pretty intense, so there is a big contrast between the shaded areas. It's important to see how the different body parts overlap each other creating shaded areas, such as on her tummy, which is on the opposite side of the light source and is totally dark.

Flat Colors

We'll begin coloring our cat with light, harmonious colors. We've decided to give her a tanned skin, which contrasts with her light-colored hair and eyes, and combines to give her a wild look. On the other hand, we've given her a furry, purple dress so it looks like she's made of an artificial material, since she's not really a cat and it's only a costume.

Shading

We'll shade the drawing following the direction marked by our highlighting, making sure we adapt the shadows to the anatomy and texture. So when we want to convey the furriness of her outfit, we'll use a sharp-pointed shadow contour with various little points around it, following the contour of the hair, which wasn't first drawn with lines.

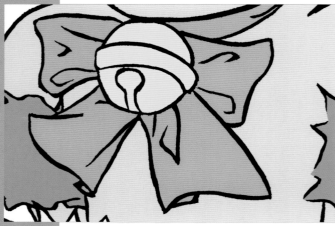

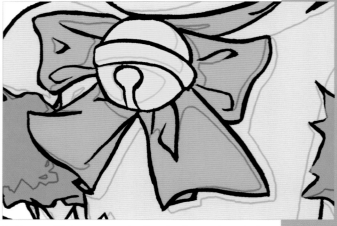

1. The process of shaping color is simple. First we'll paint a base color which will serve as an intermediate tone. It's advisable to choose a soft color that isn't very saturated.

2. Next we'll choose a color for shading and mark the areas where we'll use this tone, which will be darker and slightly more saturated.

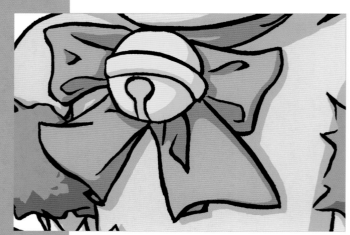

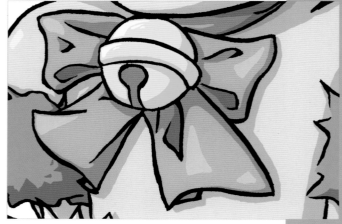

3. Now we'll fill in the areas we've marked. It's important that the shapes of the shadows match the material that's created them.

4. Lastly, we'll add highlights to areas with the most light. These will be lighter and shinier depending on how much light is reflected off the material we're painting. This way we obtain different textures.

Finishing Touches

We'll mark some highlights, such as on her skin, giving her the kind of shiny texture that comes with being tanned. Lastly, we'll mark the outline of the shadow the girl casts on the floor. This helps us position our figure better. We'll complete the drawing by adding a lighter patch of color on the wall.

Candy Girl

Candy has been produced in Japan ever since the *Heian* period and is just as popular as in the rest of the world. But as far as we're concerned, in the collective *manga* fantasy candies are synonymous with the kind of innocence portrayed by *Magical Girls*. Since the very beginnings of *manga* and *anime*, the *Magical Girl* genre has always been one of the most important and profitable. It's a genre aimed at a predominantly female audience, which is more or less acquainted with likable series such as *Magical Emi*, by Studio Pierrot; *Sailormoon* by Naoko Takeuchi; or the more recent *CardCaptor Sakura* by CLAMP, which feature innocent girls and teenagers with pure hearts, who possess magical powers with which they can fight back against the bad guys. They are always easily identified by their clothing: bright, lively colors, frilled skirts, lots of bows... Doesn't that remind you of candy wrapping?

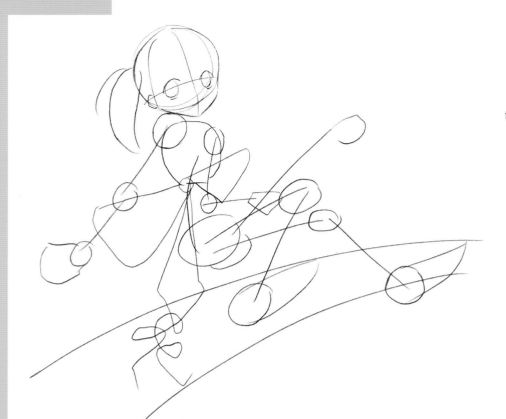

Shape

In the first place, we'll sketch out what the illustration is going to look like. In this case we have only one central figure, a girl with a magic wand in the midst of a moment of action. Floating on air, she's transported across the sky on a rainbow. It's a classic triangular-shaped composition, seen from a slightly low-angle perspective.

Volume

Now let's give the figure some volume. In order to do this we'll have to take into account the point of view we've chosen. In this case, a low-angle perspective (we're looking upwards at the action). Although it's not a very pronounced angle, we can see the underside of the girl's tush, as well as the bottom of the foot nearest us. We mustn´t forget the direction of the volume in each instance.

Anatomy

Now let's give the drawing a bit more detail. We can see how the girl's entire body reflects the tension of the moment; her extremities, arms and feet, as well as her trunk are in a rigid and uncomfortable position. On the other hand, we've given her a look of surprise or disbelief on account of the situation she's experiencing.

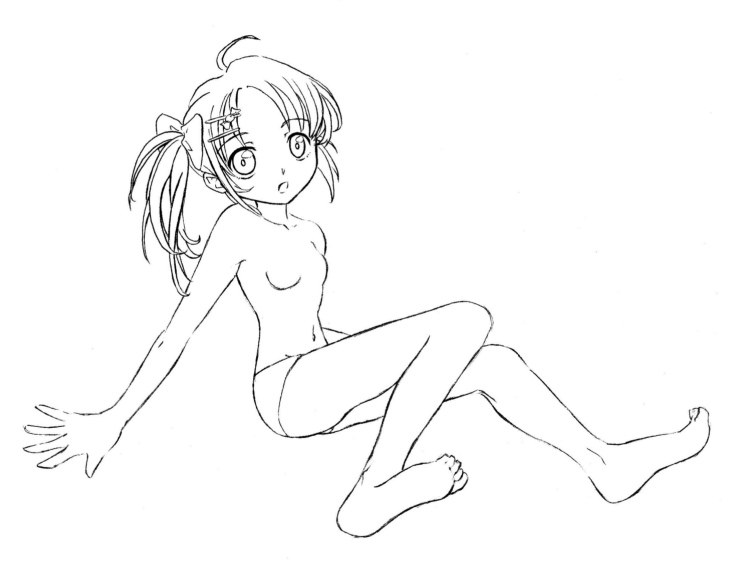

Final Sketch

We'll dress her up in clothes and fashion accessories that bring candies to mind. Her dress is bulky, tied at the ends with ribbons, forming angular wrinkles that imitate materials such as cellophane. A giant bow, such as that of a box of candies, wraps around her waist. She has chewing gum balls on her shoes as well as on her various bows, not to mention her that her magic wand is made of candy.

Lighting

We've decided that the lighting will come from in front of the girl. With this base, we can see how to distribute our shading. But the most important aspect of the drawing is the lighting, since our success in transmitting the type of smooth, shiny material we've dressed her up in totally depends on it. Highlights in these areas will be few and far between, but very intense.

Flat Colors

As usual, flat colors give a lot of brightness and low saturation. We've colored the figure with different colors, but tried to maintain a smooth chromatic harmony. Once again, we've attempted to use the idea of candies and their variety of colors, and that's why we've basically painted our character in tones of red, purple and yellow.

Shading

We'll shade just as we planned on doing in the previous steps, keeping in mind the figure's frontal illumination. Shadows for materials with shiny and rigid textures have irregular, angular shapes, while shadows for matt textures such as her skin or hair, are smooth and run parallel to the contour lines.

1. In order to give our figure greater tension we've made the direction lines which form each of the parts in the image cross each other as much as possible. For example, the direction of her trunk perpendicularly crosses the bow around her waist.

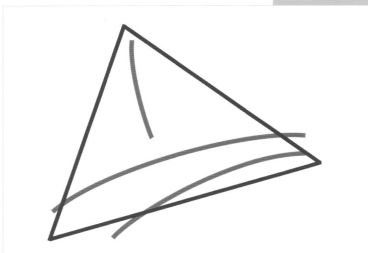

2. If we focus on the two main directions that give the figure structure, her trunk and the rainbow, we'll see them form an equilateral triangle. A guarantee that an illustration works well is when it fits into an easily identifiable geometric figure.

3. When giving the figure structure we mustn't forget the parts that are hidden under clothes or covered by other parts of the body because they're still there. For example, we should pay attention to the girl's left arm, since the position and perspective of the candy wand depend on it.

Finishing Touches

Lastly, we'll complete the drawing by adding highlights and providing a background. We'll pinpoint a few intense, irregular-shaped highlights for the shiny areas we described earlier. Highlights are not necessary for matt areas, such as her stockings. The rainbow completes the composition just as we saw in the previous steps, in addition to giving the drawing greater expression and a dreamy, magical air.

Baby Doll

In Japan, collecting the different types of classic porcelain dolls our mothers and grandmothers played with has more or less become a social and cultural institution. However, this craze hasn't just affected the world of collector's items but has actually gone on to splash the fashion world with a phenomenon better known as *Lolitas*, an urban tribe with its own lifestyle that can be divided into lots of sub-genres, such as "gothic" *Lolitas* and "sweet" *Lolitas*. Proponents of this esthetic are easily recognizable: young girls wearing clothes inspired by the Victorian era or rococo, with wide skirts, lace stockings, platform shoes, bows and lots of fashion accessories such as hats and parasols. In the worlds of *manga* and *anime* there are lots of series that rely on this esthetic, the most popular of these perhaps being *Rozen Maiden*, by Peach-Pit or series such as *Candy Candy* and *Georgie* by the *mangaka* Yumiko Igarashi.

Shape

The outline used for this illustration is simple. We have a three-quarter shot of a girl (the only parts outside the drawing are those beneath the knees). She is seen from a three-quarters view (halfway between a full-frontal view and a profile view), holding a parasol in her hands. So, rather than the action of the moment, the important thing in this drawing is her outfit and the finer details.

Volume

We'll give the figure volume by paying careful attention to the spread of her skirt and the ringlets of hair falling on her shoulders. Due to its complexity, the volume of the parasol is just as important. We'll have to make sure we don't draw it in the wrong position so it doesn't look strange. Her hands should hold the parasol firmly but subtly, so we should be careful we don't draw an overemphasized volume.

Anatomy

It's important to draw her collarbone correctly as we'll be using it as a reference in order to determine the central line that will be crossing her entire body, serving as an axis marking the exact size and location of her breasts, waist and hips. All this will help us later on when we draw her costume, since it's very well-cut and we need to adapt it to fit the girl's body properly.

Final Sketch

For her costume we've found inspiration in rococo fashion. The upper part is well-cut, with bulging sleeves that finish in a skirt with a wide swirl decorated with lace edging and bows. For the parasol, which is probably the most difficult part of the drawing, we've used a photograph of a real one seen from the same position. Using real images as references give our drawings greater credibility.

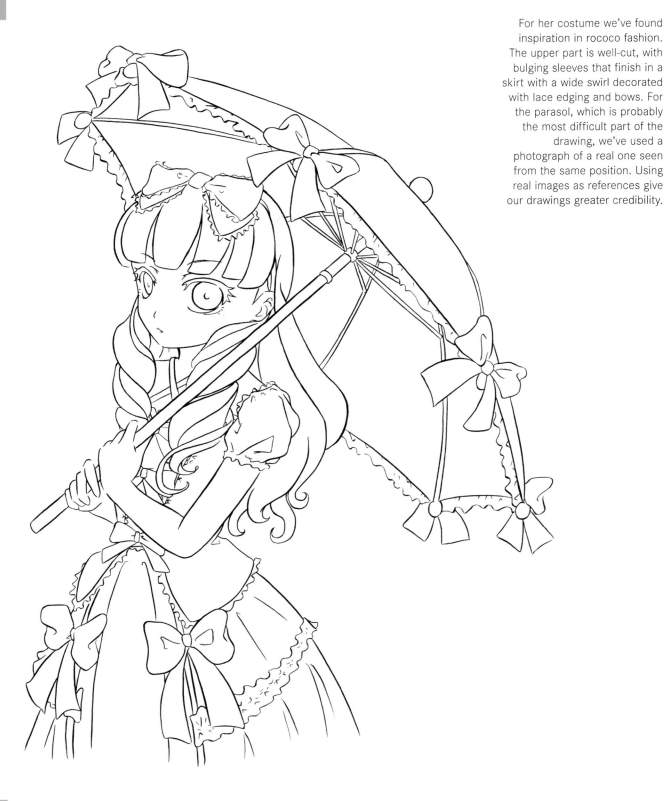

Lighting

We've decided to have the light come from in front of the girl, lighting up her face. Shadows will be drawn according to the position of the light source, paying special attention to the shadow the parasol casts on her head and on the back part of her hair. As far as the highlights are concerned, they'll be intense on the hair and skin, but not so much on her clothing since the fabrics are of a matt texture.

Flat Colors

Once again we'll find inspiration in rococo fashion when choosing the colors of her clothes. We've chosen different tones of crimson red to combine throughout. Since we're dealing with such a soft tonal range, we've painted the background sky blue to make the task a bit easier. For example, had we done it the other way around, the parasol, with its white base, would not be differentiated from the background.

Shading

We'll begin by applying a uniform layer of shading throughout the figure, all the while paying attention to where the light is coming from. Making use of a photograph of a rose as reference, we've drawn its silhouette and designed a pattern for the skirt and parasol. The rose is a simple design that combines perfectly with our drawing and helps give it a little more detail.

1. For the sky background we'll paint a large area of light blue and, with a darker tone, mark the silhouettes of the clouds with short, vaporous brush strokes. Lastly, we'll downgrade the entire painting, from darker to lighter tones, simulating atmospheric pressure.

2. We'll choose a lighter second tone for the clouds, but without it being white, and continue shaping the silhouette we've already marked. We'll use real photographs of the sky for reference in order to draw the shapes of the clouds correctly.

3. We'll choose white to polish up the cloud silhouettes with light, opaque brushstrokes. The number of strokes we'll make and the time spent on each of them will determine how realistic our sky will look in the end.

4. In order to place the image in the background of the illustration, first we should think about what it's going to look like. We'll reuse the silhouette of the rose pattern and, as if it were a glass window, we'll stick our sky on top of it. This rounds out our composition.

Finishing Touches

We'll add the background to the figure and apply a second layer of shadows wherever we feel it appropriate. Then we'll make sure that the rose-shaped silhouette we've put in the background on the left side of the image matches well with the silhouette on the parasol on the right side, balancing our illustration. Lastly, we'll add some highlights to her hair, eyes and cheeks.

Angel

An angel is an ethereal, divine being, created with the sole purpose of serving God. Contrary to popular belief, these beings are not only found in the Christian religion, but also in Judaism and Islam, in other words, the three main monotheistic religions. So what relationship do they have with Japan, and, more specifically, with the world of *manga*? Mythology has always been the main source of inspiration when creating stories. Fascination with these being in particular, which are generally asexual and have human bodies equipped with wings, is evident throughout the world of comics. Their figure transmits the concepts of purity and innocence, which are always associated with the color white, but it's for that very same reason that they are also associated with sin, giving way to the morbid idea of the fallen angel. Some of the most famous *mangas* featuring angels are *Angel Sanctuary* from the *mangaka* Kaori Yuki, and *Wish* by the CLAMP Quartet.

Shape

We'll portray our character kneeling on the ground, with her back straight and her face turned towards us. Her hands are tied behind her back with a bow wrapped around both of her wrists. The two ends of the rope spill onto the floor and make their way to the forefront of the illustration. At the same time, two large wings come out of her back and appear to be opening.

Volume

We don't see the girl from a side-angle, but from an almost three-quarter view from behind, so we'll mark the volumes of her back, as well as her shoulders, from which her two arms fall. We'll also make sure we portray the kneeling position correctly, correctly superimposing her thighs, knees and legs. Generally speaking, we must always take the subtle low-angle perspective into consideration.

Anatomy

Positioning her hands tied behind her back, with her arms tensed, makes her shoulders move slightly forward, raised and closer together. This way she can hold her posture. On the other hand, her erect body moves her trunk forwards, making it stick out significantly. Her feet which are also tense, follow the same direction as her arms.

Final Sketch

A nightgown with loose sleeves, bows and ruffles, accompanied by a sweet smile, give our character an innocent, childlike attitude. On the other hand, the shortness of her gown, the garters and, especially, the leather boots, make us imagine she has another, secondary, more mysterious personality. With such a subtle knot tying her hands so strongly together, we can't help but wonder why this angel has been denied her freedom.

Lighting

We'll place an intense light in the upper left part of the image, behind the figure. This way we'll highlight her face, revealing her expression, while practically the rest of her body remains in shadow. However, so we aren't left with a drawing that is too somber, we'll use a reverberation technique, through which we'll sketch a thread of light right on the border, just as you would see an object that's against the light.

Flat Colors

As we said before, the figure has a dual personality, so we'll be choosing colors accordingly. Tones like light pastel blue, crimson and yellow, for her nightgown, bows and hair, respectively; with bolder and colder colors like dark brown and purple for her boots and garters. Other elements such as the floor and wings remain white, at least for now.

Shading

Following the pattern we've defined in the previous steps, now we'll color in the shaded areas. We'll choose those colors that contrast with their respective flat colors in order to intensify the lighting effect. In addition, we've added hexagonal shapes to give our character's stockings texture and make them more interesting.

1. We'll focus on the composition of the illustration. We find two main axes: the line marking the horizon and the line marking the direction of her body. Visually, our attention goes to the area where the two axes cross each other, so that's where we'll place the most important elements: the boots and the bow that binds her hands.

2. We'll make our image more dynamic if we slightly turn it on its axis. This way we'll also achieve a sort of circular effect that matches the direction marked by her wings, and the feathers surrounding the central figure.

Finishing Touches

We'll finish the drawing with a secondary shadow tone in specific areas that will serve to intensify the lighting effect. Since we have such narrow reverberation areas, we won't be adding any highlights. Lastly, we'll finish the illustration with a colorful glass window on the wall and a shadow on the floor. We'll also erase the horizon line since we have enough elements marking the image's perspective.

TRADITIONAL

Samurai

Ninja

Kunoichi

Temple Guardians

Geisha

Yukata

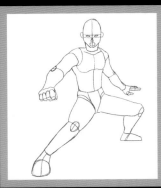

Samurai

The *samurai* is hands down the greatest icon from Japanese culture. *Samurais* were a class of warriors that were governed by *bushido*, also known as the *Way of the Warrior*, a code of honor that demanded loyalty and honor until the day they died. The *katana* is the weapon used by a *samurai*, a single-edged, slightly-curved sabre that is perfect for attacking on horseback. In the world of *manga samurais* are often used to tell epic and legendary tales. Series like *Rurouni Kenshin*, *Samurai Deeper Kyo* and *Samurai Champloo* are examples, but perhaps the most famous has been *Kozure Okami*, a *manga* created by the writer Kazuo Koike and the artist Goseki Kojima, which is about a *ronin* (an outlaw *samurai*) that wanders around the country with his son Daigoro. It's incredibly popular in Japan where they actually went on to make six films starring these two characters.

Shape

In this case, we're going to draw a *samurai* from the front, in a defensive stance. The position of his arms and legs is very important. The pose is going to be based on flexed legs and a torso positioned so as to put the hand holding the *katana* in the foreground, and his left arm in the background. This arm is going to be the one that will help us emphasize his defensive position.

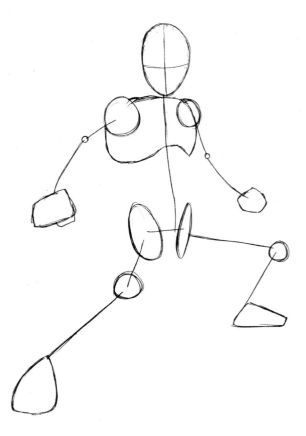

Volume

We're going to use volume to define the shape of his hands, which play an instrumental role in this illustration. The right hand holds the *katana* tightly. The positioning of his left hand defines his defensive stance. The positioning of his feet, which rest entirely on the floor, will serve as a resting point that will help us draw the rest of his leg and define the foreshortening that will be best for representing this tense moment.

Anatomy

A *samurai* is a warrior, and as such, he should have the necessary strength and resistance for combat. For this we'll draw a person with muscles that aren't overdeveloped, although we will make sure they are big enough to convey the idea that we're dealing with an experienced warrior. His facial gesture should transmit decisiveness, since a *samurai* shows complete concentration when in combat.

Final Sketch

We'll finish the drawing by adding complex armor. This will also serve to distinguish him as a *samurai*, probably working for some emperor. We must take the finer details of the era into account, such as the fastenings holding the rudimentary shin guards in place. We'll also add the *katana*, which will be placed in the foreground, where it will help give the image greater depth.

Lighting

We'll draw our character just as the sun is setting, a typical scene with diffused light. The point of light, the sun, is positioned just behind the character and adds epic drama to the scene. Whenever the main light source is positioned behind the central element of an illustration, the shadow contrasts won't be very marked, as we can see with this *samurai*.

Flat Colors

We'll paint the metallic parts of his armor and the rest of his clothes, with cold colors, but with a touch of black. In contrast, we'll use warm colors on his breastplate and on details such as the fastenings holding his shin guards and the tie which wraps around the handle of his *katana* and sheath. We'll use a bluish-gray on the *katana's* blade in order to differentiate it from the armor's metallic parts.

Shading

Now we'll draw the shadows which will help add volume to each piece of armor, such as his breastplate, which has a smooth shape thanks to its rounded lines, or the shoulder pads, which are constructed with much more angular shapes. It's very important to differentiate the shadows from the clothes, which have a matt texture. This means they won't reflect light the way the armor will.

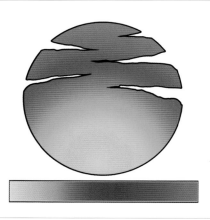

1. Create a circle and fill it with diminishing colors based on those of a sunset.

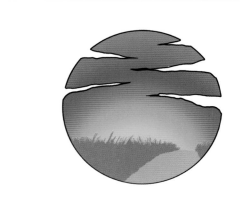

2. Add the base colors for what will be a dirt and grass pathway.

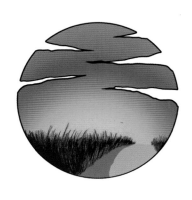

3. Create the shaded grass and pathway by using quick movements with a fine brush.

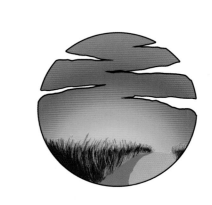

4. Finish by adding highlights to the upper part of the undergrowth so as to give it some volume.

Finishing Touches

For this final step we're going to add a yellow tone to simulate direct sunlight. This will help us mark the exact positioning of his body with respect to the reader and accentuate the illustration's volume. We'll finish by drawing the background, which will directly show the light source and, at the same time, serve as a point of reference that positions our character.

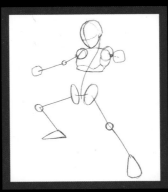

Ninja

Ninjas are agents who have come to master the art of *ninjutsu*. These agents have been trained to go unrecognized in almost any environment thanks to spectacular hiding techniques that allow them to complete whatever spy missions they've been assigned. However, *ninjas* are not only known for their stealth, they're also known for their ability to handle all kinds of weapons and for their hand-to-hand combat skills, as these are areas in which they are true experts. *Ninjas* can be easily recognized by their attire, which consists of dark clothes that allow them to hide amongst the shadows of the night. They also keep their faces covered. *Ninjas* are used quite regularly in the world of Japanese entertainment. Good examples can be found in *anime* series like *Ninja Scroll* and *Hattori Ninja-Kun*, video-games like *Shinobi* and *Ninja Gaiden* and even in films like *Red Shadow*.

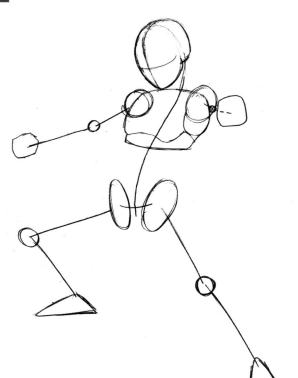

Shape

Ninjas are action heroes, so they are always ready to jump into action. In this case we've chosen a front view. The character will be positioned at the top of a *Shintoist* temple. Since he's on the top of a slanted roof, one of his legs will be flexed and the other will project towards us, as will his left arm.

Volume

We'll use volume to determine the position of his arms. Taking advantage of the bent wrist that's holding the sword, we'll actually make it look like it's an extension of his arm. The left arm is easier to draw since his hand almost completely covers it. We can also see because of the slope how his left foot isn't visible from the front but from a high-angle view.

Anatomy

The character is in a state of tension, so his body has to be rigid. We'll make him more dynamic by slightly exaggerating the arch of his back, with his center of gravity behind his waist. The character is alert, so he should have a serious expression that takes its strength from his eyes and the shape of his eyebrows, since his nose and mouth won't be visible in our final illustration.

Final Sketch

We'll dress the character in a typical ninja uniform, but we'll give him a personal touch by adding some characteristic protective elements, such as metallic bracelets and a chest protector. We'll draw a small yin yang on it to give it that oriental touch. Let's also add some small dragon ears and tusks to his head area. As a final detail we'll draw a large flowing handkerchief around his neck that will give him some movement.

Lighting

The moon is what illuminates this drawing, and it's located behind the character. From the artist's perspective, having the light source so close means that the differences in the shaded and lit areas should be quite obvious to the reader. This can be achieved by maximizing the contrast between these areas and emphasizing it as much as possible.

Flat Colors

We'll paint our character's clothes with saturated, off-colors with a touch of black that gives them a hint of darkness. Since we're dealing with a *ninja*, and it's nighttime, any colors should incline towards black. We can give the illustration greater contrast by painting his handkerchief and belt red, while maintaining our general tendency towards black.

Shading

By keeping the light source
behind our character we can
take the opportunity to shape
his clothes, and begin
visualizing what his volume will
look like. We have to consider
that a shadow will behave in
different ways depending on the
type of material being reflected.
While shadows on the clothes
serve to accentuate their folds,
the sword lends a metallic
texture.

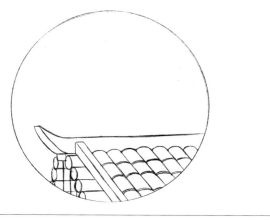

1. We'll draw a simple sketch of the idea we want to paint.

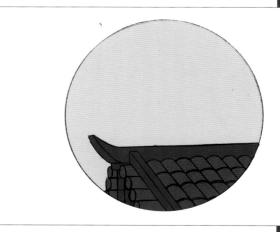

2. Let's work with color toning so that the contrast between the moon and the building is very clear.

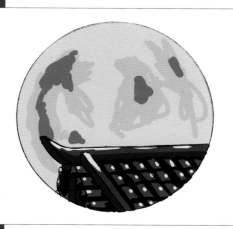

3. We'll add the shadows and highlights appropriate for each texture. It's important to always have references at hand.

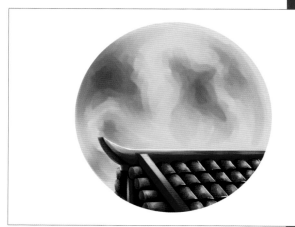

4. Now let's shape the shadows and lights we have mentioned in the previous step, adding new tones and lighting as we deem them necessary.

Finishing Touches

Once the character and the background have been joined, we'll add the finishing touches to the shading and lighting so that they match perfectly, and don't look like they come from different drawings. We'll finish our illustration by projecting the character's shadow over the background, keeping in mind that it shouldn't be completely opaque.

Kunoichi

Female *ninjas* are known as *kunoichi*. They are just as fearsome as their male counterparts, although they have the handicap of appearing less strong than them. And we say "appear", because they certainly know how to use their femininity to plot their deception and kill their victims without raising suspicion. One of their favorite tricks is to wear tight outfits that succeed in distracting their enemy while they proceed to beat them to a bloody pulp as they just stand there looking at them as if in a trance. In a traditionally chauvinistic society such as Ancient Japan, *kunoichi* enjoyed a similar status to men. We have examples of *kunoichis* in the world of videogames, such as *Taki* from *Soulcalibur*, or in the case of *anime* we can find series like *2x2=Shinobuden* where *ninjas* and *kunoichis* come together in humorous situations, and there are also others that are more epic such as *Basilisk*.

Shape

We'll use a front view, with our *kunoichi* waving her sword menacingly. Our character tries to maintain her distance from her enemy by stretching her arm towards us. This way it is the reader who is in fact the enemy. We've chosen the moment just before the *kunoichi* uses the sword, thus maintaining the tension of not knowing exactly when she's going to strike.

Volume

We'll use volume to define the layout of the pose. We'll draw her right hand by using simple shapes which, at the same time, serve to force the position of her fingers and make her hand more dynamic. The position of her right foot, together with her flexed left leg, give the image greater depth, and at the same time add a sense of volume.

Anatomy

We'll contrast the rigid pose of her body and arms with the dynamics of her hair, which helps to give the drawing movement. In this case we have to work extra hard when drawing in detail the way her eyes look and the arch of her eyebrows, in order to transmit and maintain the tension of the moment. After all, she's a *kunoichi* which means that her face will be covered and we won't be able to rely on her mouth to convey her emotions.

Final Sketch

We'll finish the drawing by giving her a tight outfit. We'll take advantage to add some bindings on her arms, which will help accentuate her movement when the time comes to brandish her sword and keep her distance from her enemy. Although in this case we can see her hair, *kunoichis* have to be careful to keep their identity well-hidden, which is why we've added a hood to her outfit.

Lighting

With the help of an almost zenithal light source coming from somewhere above the character, we'll mark her volume according to her outfit. The clothes she's wearing are made of a shiny material that is similar to silk, a material that reflects more light than, for example, the bindings, which are made of an absorbent material.

Flat Colors

Kunoichis must remain hidden just like *ninjas*, so when it comes to their clothes, dark colors must also predominate. In this particular case, we'll add little bits of color to our character's hair, her bindings and belt. Even so, we must always, make sure we give these colors a touch of black too so they match those of the rest of the drawing.

Shading

We'll use shading to define the texture of her clothes and other accessories. At the same time we must define the shape of her sword and the volume of her bindings, which will help us portray her arm movement. Little by little we'll be adding the finer details, such as the shadow of her mouth and the volume of her nose, which is visible beneath the fabric covering her face.

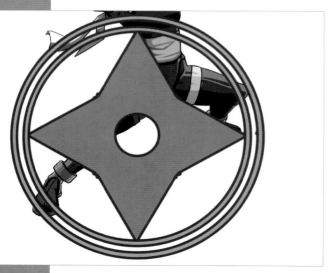

1. We'll make the floor a little more interesting by drawing a simple rosette on it. This is based on the famous *ninjutsu* art known as *shuriken*.

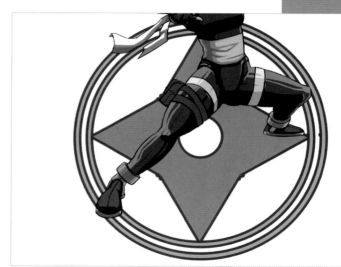

2. Once it has been placed at foot level, we'll place it behind the character in order to begin putting it at the right angle.

3. We'll shape it and place it at a perfect angle so that it creates depth and volume. This way we'll make sure it doesn't look like our character is on a flat surface.

Finishing Touches

We'll add the finishing lighting and shading touches depending on the textures we're painting. We'll make her outfit look like latex by blending in a lighter tone. We'll also at this point add light to her hair, thus giving it more dynamic movement. Finally, we'll project the shadow of the rosette to increase the feeling that the character is on a solid surface.

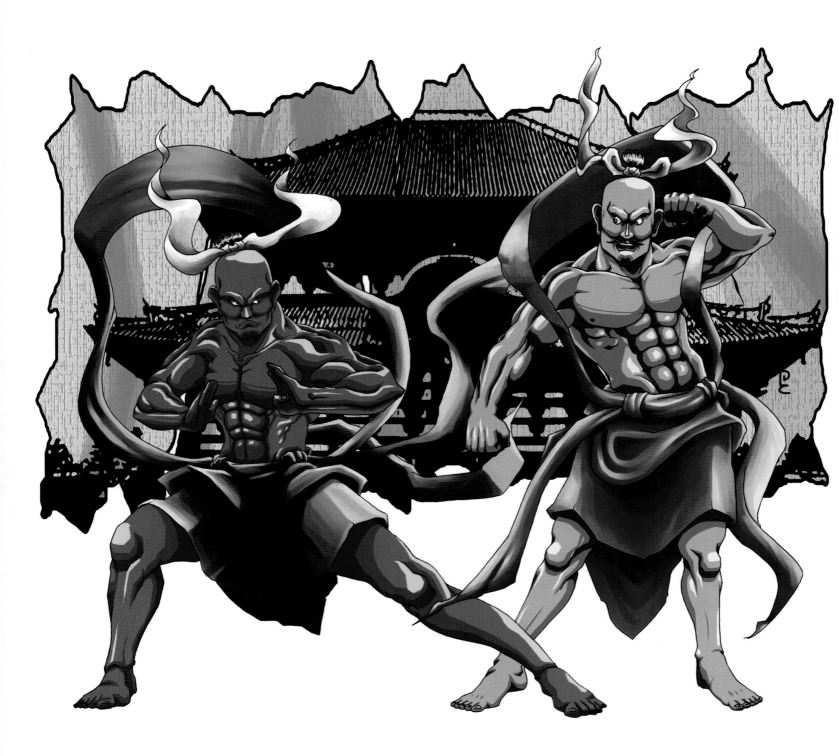

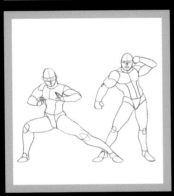

Temple Guardians

The *Nio* kings (translated as the *Benevolent Kings*) are two guardians that are said to have originally come from India to protect Buddha on his travels throughout that country. Agyo, the guardian with his mouth open, represents the sound of the first *devanaagarii* in Sanskrit, which sounds like an "a". Ungyo, who has his mouth shut, represents the last *devanaagarii* in Sanskrit, which sounds like "un". The two guardians represent the concepts of birth and death, alfa and omega, the beginning and end. They are also known as *Kongo*, *Kongou*, *Kongo Rikishi*, *Kong Rikishi* and *Shitsukong-shin*. Their statues are found at the entrance of Buddhist temples, one on the right, the other on the left, since they are said to scare away bad spirits, demons and thieves. These guardians have made appearances in *anime* series like *Gantz*, *Saint Seiya* and *Hokuto No Ken*.

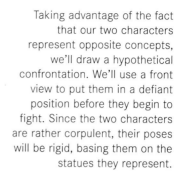

Shape

Taking advantage of the fact that our two characters represent opposite concepts, we'll draw a hypothetical confrontation. We'll use a front view to put them in a defiant position before they begin to fight. Since the two characters are rather corpulent, their poses will be rigid, basing them on the statues they represent.

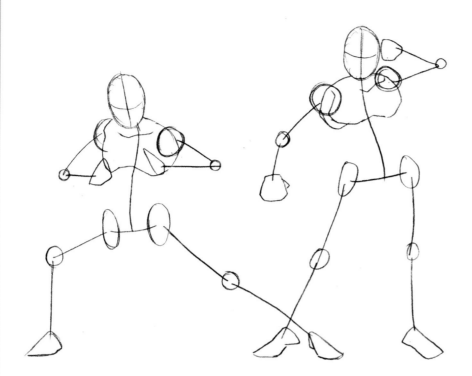

Volume

In this particular exercise, volume will help us shape their muscles and the position of the Benevolent Kings' arms and legs. We'll define the position of their feet using simple shapes that will help us keep the two figures on the same plane, so the reader can see them from a front view.

Anatomy

Our two characters are very muscular, so we'll have to get references from muscle and fitness magazines. We won't emphasize all the muscles of their bodies as we don't want to overload the drawing unnecessarily. We'll stylize their waists to take a bit of the rigidity out of their bodies and give them some mobility. We'll draw one of them with an open mouth, and the other with a closed mouth, but both of them will have knitted brows.

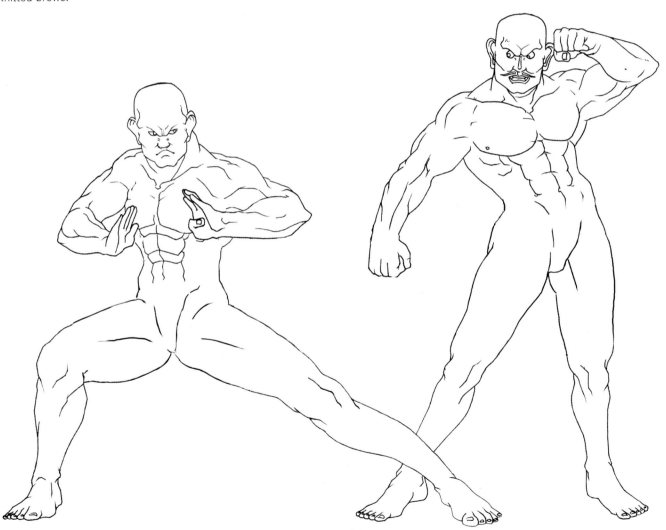

Final Sketch

Since we're drawing muscular characters, in this case we won't be dealing with much clothing. However, this doesn't mean that their clothing is any less important than other areas of the illustration. We'll draw skirts with the necessary folds so we don't lose volume or the position of their feet. We'll use the rest of their wardrobe to give the characters greater presence.

Lighting

We'll mark our characters' shadows keeping a zenithal light source in mind. It will help us to use a strong contrast that will also serve to maintain their fearsome and threatening looks. We'll use a less evident contrast on their clothes, which we'll paint in a matt hue that doesn't attract too much attention, but which also doesn't compete with the color of their flesh either.

Flat Colors

In order to make the difference between the characters more evident, we'll use a cold color like blue for one of them, and a much warmer color like red for the other. We'll also create contrast between the characters and their clothing, using tones that contrast with their skin color: in short, one of the characters will have a cold skin-color and warm-colored clothing and the other will have a warm skin-color but cold-colored clothing.

Shading

Just as when studying their anatomies, at this stage it will be very helpful to have as many references to hand as possible so we can shape their muscles as we go about shading, obtaining the kind of volume that's as correct as possible. In addition, we mustn't forget to pay attention to the shadows of the clothes, which will help enrich the illustration.

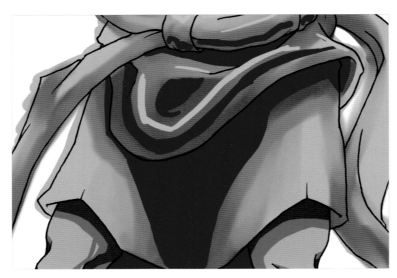

1. Based on the shadows we've added in the previous step, we'll add light colors that will also serve to brighten the illustrations, and darker colors which will help give clothing more consistency.

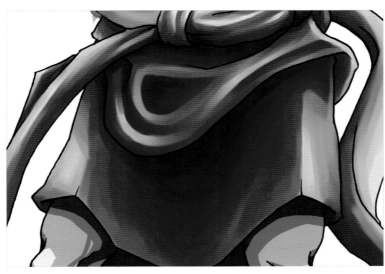

2. We'll blend colors using our light source as reference, applying dark or light tones as we find necessary until we achieve a consistent texture for their clothing.

Finishing Touches

We'll finish by adding the final highlights and shadows. These will help to accentuate their volume and muscles, the main prop for this illustration. We'll finish painting their clothing with a matt finish that contrasts with the glossy finish of the characters. We'll top it all off with a background that completes the composition.

Geisha

Geishas initially emerged to play a role in the entertainment world. Although it might seem strange to us now, at first the majority of *geishas* were men who dedicated themselves to the art of entertaining their clients at parties and social reunions. Over time, women began to declare themselves *geishas* and their clients were mainly men. They offered services such as story-telling, dancing and music. It didn't take long for female *geishas* to outnumber their male counterparts, until one day the latter disappeared altogether. Nowadays the term *geisha* is solely used for women. *Geishas* are one of the greatest Japanese cultural icons and, although not as prevalent as in the past, even today, it's possible to see them strolling the streets of Japanese cities, especially in the *Gyon* neighborhood of Kyoto.

Shape

We're going to put this character in the typical Japanese sitting fashion known as *seiza*. This *seiza* position shows respect at the same time as a certain submissiveness. The frontal view allows us to see the *geisha* in a natural pose, showing her appreciation by stretching her arm with an open handed gesture of friendliness towards the person sitting in front of her, in this case, the reader.

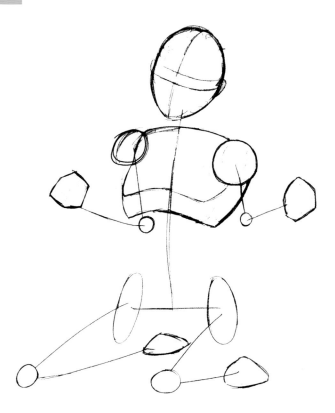

Volume

At this stage we'll sort out the complicated areas, such as her left hand, which is holding the parasol. A simple bending of her wrist will give her a more natural and less rigid look. This is the complete opposite of what occurs with the other hand, where we'll force the position of her fingers to give them a slight sense of movement, as if we were drawing her at the exact moment when she stretches her arm.

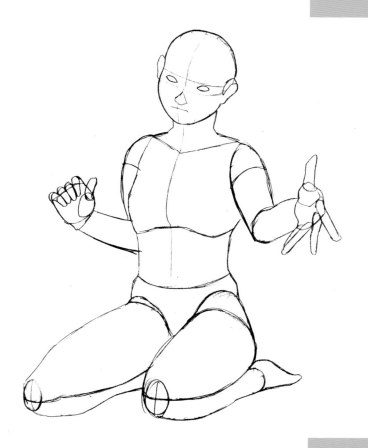

Anatomy

Since the position of her trunk is pretty natural, the strength of the image lies in her hands. With a friendly gesture her right hand invites us get closer to her. The person the *geisha* is addressing could be her partner (in Japan lovers are drawn beneath a parasol instead of surrounded by hearts). But we'll sketch a smile which shows indifference just to leave the reader in doubt.

Final Sketch

We'll finish the drawing adding the typical *geisha* outfit, the *kimono*, which we'll draw with all its accessories, such as the *obi*, the sash covering her waist. We must also consider the wrinkles formed by the long sleeves and the position of her legs. We'll add a typical Japanese parasol made of wood and fabric. This kimono is a much fuller garment in comparison to the *yukata* which we drew in the previous exercise.

Lighting

We'll use a zenithal light source as reference (for example, the sun), which will also serve to project the shadow of the parasol on the floor. Since the character itself is beneath the parasol, this light source won't be affecting her, so we'll focus on the shadows caused by the wrinkles and folds of her clothes.

Flat Colors

Geishas are characterized by the *kimonos* they wear and the bright colors that attract the viewer's attention and contrast with the white paint that covers their face. We'll use saturated colors for her make-up and a gray base for her hair, which we'll use to our advantage and give volume for a more natural effect.

Shading

We'll give the character more volume by making use of the folds and wrinkles. At the same time, we'll be giving texture to the clothes and other accessories in the drawing. Paying attention to the zenithal lighting, we'll make it so the parasol lets a little bit of light pass through it. So, while the parasol won't have shadows, its spokes will. While we're at it, let's give them some volume.

1. We'll give the *kimono* a floral pattern that will serve to enrich the design of her clothes.

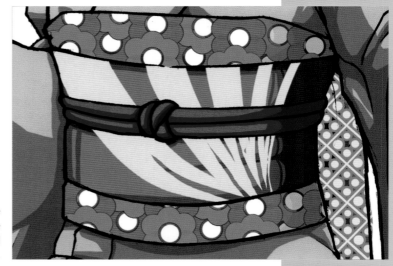

2. We'll place the design in the areas of the clothes we've already chosen and then we'll cut them out.

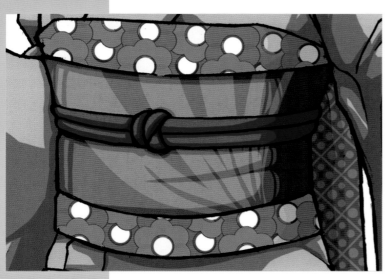

3. In order to take advantage of the shadows we created earlier, and so the colors don't clash, we'll minimize the opacity of the patterns and make them transparent.

Finishing Touches

We'll finish placing patterns on the clothes wherever we think necessary. These should be painted with saturated colors so they don't look like those of the clothes and contrast with them. We'll add the final touches of shading that will enrich the lighting. Lastly, we'll make sure we've colored each and every part of the drawing.

Yukata

The *yukata* is a cotton piece of clothing worn by women that is similar to a *kimono*. Normally it's used in the summer, the season when they celebrate festivals like *tanabata* (which is celebrated on the seventh day of the seventh month of the year) and *bon-odori*. Since it's such a light piece of clothing, the *yukata* is only used in the warmest months of the year. Unlike the *kimono*, the *yukata* doesn't require that you wear anything beneath it, such as a *nagajuban*. The *yukata* is often used in *manga* to tell the reader that the story takes place during the summer and, very probably, during the celebration of one of the summer festivals. It's a resource that's often used in the *shojo* genre, since during the *Tanabata* festival, which is similar to our Valentine's Day, lovers take the opportunity of declaring their love. This is the perfect situation for telling the more romantic *manga* stories.

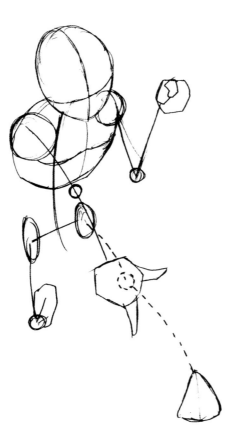

Shape

For this drawing we've chosen a moment of maximum tension, when the character is throwing hoops during a summer festival. From a front view we'll be emphasizing the position of her body in order to show a very dynamic movement. We'll exaggerate the position of the arm that's throwing so we can put it in the foreground.

Volume

In this drawing we'll use different planes to express volume. The right arm is our main reference; we'll give it volume with simple cylindrical shapes, as well as by emphasizing the position of her hand. The character's torso is our second reference, which we'll create by slightly arching her back over the resting point, which, in this case, is her left foot.

Anatomy

Here we'll use the hair to help us define the strength of the character's movement. If you look closely, her hair marks a diagonal line to her left foot, which passes through her right arm. This helps accentuate her tension. We'll show the reader that the girl is concentrating while performing the movement. But since it's just fun and games, we'll give her a more relaxed air by drawing her tongue just as she tastes her ice cream.

Final Sketch

We'll give the drawing its final details, such as the ice cream she's holding in her left hand. We'll draw it so it looks like it can fall at any moment on account of the character's exaggerated movement. The *yukata* should fit the character's position when in action. Continuing with her emblematic Japanese attire, we'll draw her some typical *geta* sandals.

Lighting

Since the action takes place during a summer festival, the light source will come from a zenithal perspective, from the attractive and colorful paper lamps that are typical at these festivals. We'll mark the shadows on the clothes with less contrasting tones because of their matt texture. We'll also bear in mind that this kind of lamp really doesn't provide a great deal of light.

Flat Colors

We'll use bright colors for the character, which will also help us contrast her with the background. We'll be using the same range of colors on the girl as we will on the scoops of ice cream, so they match well. Lastly, we'll paint her skin color reflecting Japanese beauty standards: the less tan you have the more beautiful you are. That is why we've chosen to give our character a pale skin-color.

Shading

We'll shade in our drawing based on the light source described in our lighting section. We'll pay attention to the wrinkles made by the character's position and at this point use these to our advantage to shape the volume of her hair and flesh. We'll use a dotted shading technique to create texture on the three scoops of ice cream.

1. *Yukatas* usually have patterns, although these are not as complex as those of *kimonos*. In this case we've chosen a floral motif.

2. Let's adapt the design to the correct angle and perspective of her clothing.

3. We'll adjust the design, erasing excess bits. We'll repeat this on other areas of the clothing, always respecting direction and the folds that are created.

Finishing Touches

We'll add the final objects, such as the hoop, which we'll place in the foreground. We'll draw it with a thick line in order to accentuate its position. We'll paint its shadows while following its circumference, which will help us make it look like it is spinning. Then we'll add highlights, and lastly, we'll add the background, which is made using off-colors and which places us in the scene that is unfolding.

ACTION

Otaku

SD Hero

Gang Member

Adventure Woman

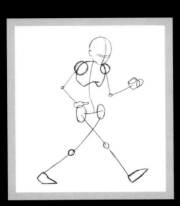

Otaku

What would a *manga* character be if there was nobody by his side to help him? And especially, that computer expert friend that helps him through the difficult times, while at the same being an avid *manga* reader. Normally we're talking about a silent friend who spends the day in front of the computer or devouring books of *manga*. We're talking about the *otaku*. *Otakus* are known outside Japan as fans of *manga*, *anime* and everything related to them, only without the negative connotation of the word in their native country. In Japan this term is usually used for those who are obsessed with their hobby, which doesn't necessarily have to be *manga- related*. They tend to have a very poor or non-existent social life. Perhaps the most famous *otaku* is Otakon, a character from the videogame series *Metal Gear Solid*, but we can find dozens of other examples in the world of *manga/anime*.

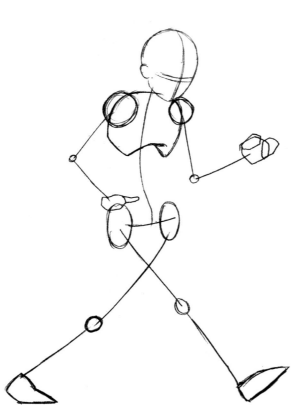

Shape

In this exercise we'll present this character in a moment of leisure. In this case we've decided his hobbies are computer programming and *manga*, so we'll draw him strolling around the *Akihabara* area, which is *otaku-paradise*. We'll draw him in a fairly ordinary position taken from a front view. We'll take into account the forward arch of his back due to the weight of his rucksack.

Volume

For this stage we'll use simple shapes to position his feet, which are crucial when it comes time to give the character movement. Apart from that, our volume study will also allow us to see the arch of his right arm, which tells us he's carrying something. We'll draw a few geometric shapes to create the right hand holding the mobile phone.

Anatomy

These characters have normal physiques, although in Japan the *otaku* concept is quite the opposite of that in the West. In the West, these characters are usually overweight and plagued by acne. In Japan they're quite thin, almost anemic. The only common feature is their glasses.

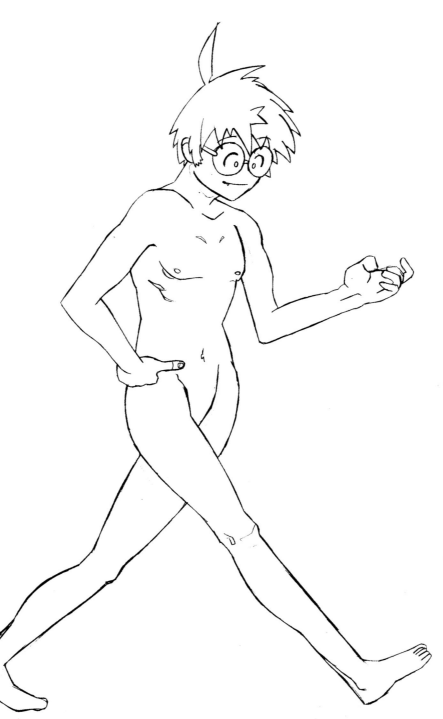

Final Sketch

We'll complete the drawing by giving him some simple clothing. The important thing about these characters is to give them a gesture of complicity with the reader. Since in this case we're drawing a fan of computer programming and *manga*, we'll put a strap on his mobile and a computer under his arm. The character's expression conveys happiness, since he's in his natural environment and he's just bought some interesting material.

Lighting

We'll rely on an entirely zenithal light source since our character is ambling along outdoors, marking the contrasts in his clothes and the wrinkles formed by the position of his legs. We should also bear in mind the shadow he projects in order for it to look like he's walking over a solid surface and not just floating in air.

Flat Colors

We'll use bright, light colors, but without too much white color. For contrast, we'll paint the boy's shirt dark gray. We have to remember that these characters spend most of their time at home in front of their computers or reading, so their skin should be as pale as possible.

Shading

We'll use shadows to begin giving the character and his clothes some volume, all the while taking into consideration the zenithal lighting we mentioned in the previous step. Shadows will help us mark the direction of his legs, which are hidden beneath his pants. Since the sun is our light source, the contrasts in his clothes shouldn't be over-exaggerated, but more uniform instead.

1. *Akihabara*, also known as *Akiba* is a place full of stores devoted to the world of electronics, videogames, merchandising and, of course, everything related to *manga* and *anime*. We'll draw a background brimming with details like illuminated signs, posters and trees and buildings covered with advertising.

Finishing Touches

We'll arrange the background of the streets of *Akihabara* behind our character. We'll add final shading touches that will help define him and the volume of his accessories, such as the white highlights on his computer. Let's also add details such as an invented software label on his bag, leading readers to believe he's bought something computer- related, and some details on his shirt that pay homage to some *anime* series.

SD Hero

What defines a hero? Generally speaking, a hero is a person that shines high above the rest in terms of idealistic values and, often has supernatural abilities. Heroes are capable of the most extraordinary accomplishments. But it's not always so easy. The way to get closer to heroes is to present them as totally mediocre characters with their most human facets; before they are able to undertake a heroic deed. Then, afterwards you show their growth and the kinds of feats which make them truly legendary. The hero is usually the one who makes all the difference, especially in the face of greater challenges, to which he never surrenders, demonstrating an unstoppable volition and unlimited passion that enable him to realize his dreams. In *manga*, the stereotype is usually a young boy or girl who has to face up to a series of events that will test their bravery, and especially, their spirit, which should be unyielding.

Shape

In order to present these characters in their most tender light, they are usually parodied, although without ridiculing them. The idea is to make them more approachable to the reader. So we'll be using SD or *superdeformed* proportions, as we try to strike a pose that shows great determination. We can show our character with his back erect, a good sign of self-confidence.

Volume

Superdeformed characters tend to be simple and rounded. We'll be keeping these general guidelines as we construct our character's pet. Giving the hero a pet he has to take care of highlights his human nature and brings him nearer to the reader. We've opted for a wolf-dog, which might not be very original, but it fits the stereotype.

Anatomy

When developing his expression we'll bear the same idea in mind as we did when designing his posture, especially when it comes to the look in his eyes. Heroes tend to show great self-confidence and determination. We can close his eyes slightly and knit his brow as if he were fixing his gaze on something. We'll draw his pet using loose, angular lines that represent his furry texture.

Final Sketch

We've chosen a very oriental look for our hero, a bit like a modern *ninja*, although this isn't really very important since heroes are timeless and don't know anything about countries or fashion. But we can resort to folklore and mythology to find heroes and fighters that can inspire our designs. Lots of heroes are warriors and carry weapons with them.

Lighting

Generally speaking, the shape of the shadows is usually sweet and rounded for *superdeformed* characters, as we can see from his skin and clothes, but when painting specific textures we don't need to do this. In the case of the dog's fur, the shadows should be painted with the same strokes used to shape its contour lines, which are a lot more angular and triangular.

Flat Colors

Choosing colors is very important here. It can be very useful to base ourselves on color symbolism when picking colors for our hero. White symbolizes purity, while red is associated with fury, danger, blood and passion. However, each culture has its nuances. Moreover, if we give our character an unusual hair or eye color it will help to make him look even more special.

Shading

Since in this case the drawing serves to introduce our character, we'll try to use a very clear lighting, with few shadows, which avoids us having to darken our character or his attire, while allowing us to show his most benevolent side. Light symbolizes good and darkness is used for evil, although it's not a rule of thumb and sometimes we can play around with this as we like.

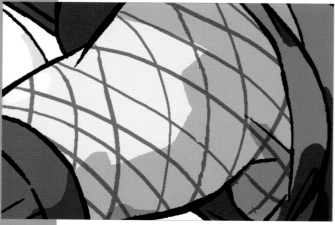

1. We'll use color to draw light netting that completes our character's attire. When drawing this kind of clothing item and accessories, we should follow the spherical volume of the body. Using color instead of black will make it lighter.

2. This combination of red and violet blends the symbolism of passion and sacrifice.

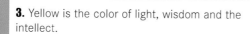

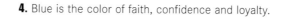

3. Yellow is the color of light, wisdom and the intellect.

4. Blue is the color of faith, confidence and loyalty.

Finishing Touches

Adding a circular yellow background is a compositional resource that also serves as a complement to the chromatic range we've been working with in this illustration. A nice exercise is to create characters based on the feelings that their colors bring out qualities. This way we're creating graphic color combinations that say things about our character's psyche.

Gang Member

A real villain has a strong following: people who are like scraps of meat to be devoured to the delight of our hero. These guys are usually big-time criminals. Often they're psychopaths or shameless killers... Just the right cards to be holding if you want to end up taking a beating at the hands of the hero of the moment. Generally these characters get together to form gangs and practice a wide range of criminal activities. They don't follow a specific fashion style. Some wear suits, some wear baggy clothes and sneakers and you can even find our favorites, the post-apocalyptic neo-fascists that dress up as radical punks. These in particular, which developed from the style popularized by the film *Mad Max*, were the image of the fearsome bad guy in *manga* and *anime* for many years. The violence of the punk movement was exploited and taken to unthought-of limits by these troublemakers who worked for the highest bidder, or simply for fun, while innocent people suffered.

Shape

We're going to draw a radical, threatening type, so we'll have to use a few different tricks if we're going to achieve this. The stance should be tough. We can even incline the character forwards, as if challenging the reader. Proportions should be disproportionate, even monstrous, since the character should instill fear and terrorize the reader.

Volume

We can play with the character's highly disproportionate proportions. In this case his body will show muscular hypertrophy, so we'll draw him with a gigantic thoracic box and shoulders. In fact, all the volumes should be gigantic in comparison to his head, which doesn't need to hold too many brain cells. Perspective should exaggerate this effect even more.

Anatomy

His body is exaggeratedly muscular on account of drugs and steroids. All his muscles are well-defined, as if they were pumped-up and thick veins cover his skin in the areas of his chest and arms. His face and expression are very important. His wide-open eyes, with their tiny-pupils, and his sinister smile help convert our character into a really terrifying monster.

Final Sketch

We've chosen the punk look for our character, so we can use a wide range of elements that will make him more aggressive. Some classic elements are Mohawks, piercings, nails, studs, enormous steel-tip boots, some military equipment, chains, old and worn clothes, etc. When put together the final result should shock the reader a little.

Lighting

In this exercise we see how we can use shading and lighting to give a drawing greater depth. The gang member's body is inclined forward, so his torso will project a shadow over the lower part of his trunk, abdominal muscles, hips and, lastly, his waist, which is practically hidden. We'll also use shading to make all his muscles stand out, exaggerating them even more.

Flat Colors

We've chosen a really loud color selection. The idea is to create an impact and make the reader feel insecure. Anybody who can wear this kind of clothing, and combine colors like these, obviously has a few screws loose. Everything about him is exaggerated, such as the tropical parrot feathers which draw the attention of everybody around him. His skin is whitish, which helps make him look sick and gloomy.

Shading

We'll draw the character respecting the shapes of each element. In other words, the feathers will be more rounded, the boots will show reflections, and the leather and metal will show the kind of highlights that are characteristic of these materials. Contrasting with the pale punk is his pet black cat with a Mohawk, which hangs from his chain, and serves as yet another histrionic touch of humor that enriches our character.

Tips and Tricks

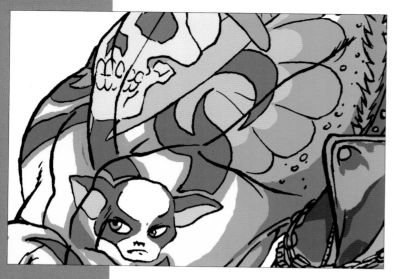

1. To paint the tattoo, first we'll paint each of its elements with a base color, trying to keep a general tone and using typical tattoo colors.

2. Next we'll draw the shadows and the rest of the color details that complete the illustrations.

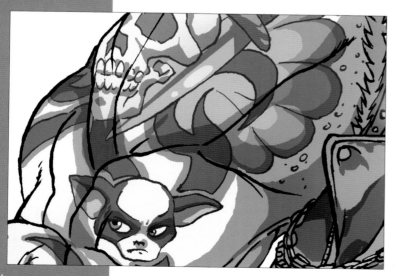

3. Finally we'll go over the tattoo's outline with a lighter color than the rest of the drawing. We'll also add a highlight on his shoulder to finish giving him the proper volume.

Finishing Touches

We'll complete all the volumes and shadows by projecting the shadows of our character onto the floor, thus giving him a good support base. When drawing shadows we must always make sure they correspond with the perspective. We've used white airbrushing to add more exaggerated highlights to metal objects such as the chains and handcuffs.

Adventure Woman

In *manga*, women play a very important role in action, adventure and fantasy stories. In fact, in lots of stories the female character is the central figure, and the man plays a secondary or supporting role. Since *manga* is aimed at a teenage audience, whether it is to please boys who are anxious to see lively heroines, or girls looking to see themselves reflected in inspiring characters, women are sure to be seen playing leading roles. These female characters are usually the ones who breathe fire into the storyline, which is why it's not strange to find women who won't hesitate in hurling themselves into an adventure, even in the face of the greatest dangers, just as masculine heroes have done for centuries in the West. Without a doubt their sex- appeal, combined with the characteristics of the traditional male hero, plays an important part in making them favorites of the public at large.

Shape

In order to capture a character's action and spirit of adventure the most important thing to do is to know how to capture the heat of the moment, the point of maximum danger and risk, the embodiment of dramatic movement. For our heroine we've chosen to show her just as she takes a giant leap forward, although any action can be good: a race, a fight, explosions, falls etc.

Volume

The next step in drawing this type of illustration is to try to give it a special focus for the action we've chosen. We have to foreshorten, use high and low angle perspectives that exaggerate the movement we're drawing. All these tricks will help fill our image with action. We've opted for a low-angle perspective that emphasizes our character's flight.

Anatomy

When drawing heroines, it's a good idea to be unbiased and draw characters that are as attractive for girls as they are for boys. They should be beautiful though not excessively so, athletic and with an attractive personality. They can be full of vitality, extroverted and very mysterious, so that we always want to know more about them. They must capture the reader's attention.

Final Sketch

Clothes are also very important for this type of character. They define their profession and can say things about their role, their tastes and their peculiarities, becoming one of the most direct ways a reader can identify with them. Many *manga* heroines set off trends among their fans, and their outfit plays an important part in this. That's why it's a good idea to make our outfit as original as possible.

Lighting

In our drawing we can use shadows in two different ways. By positioning them in the lower part of the drawing, on account of the zenithal lighting we'll give the figure weight and reinforce the notion that she's falling. But also, the shadows and tones in the foreground can be dark and saturated to accentuate the perspective even more.

Flat Colors

Once again, fantasy. We've found inspiration in military clothing such as the military-style vest, but we'll personalize it by painting it a very bright pink. Without a doubt, her unusual vest and hairstyle will become elements that will distinguish our character and make it easier to recognize her. Once we've chosen these tones we'll try to color in the rest of the elements to make them look attractive.

Shading

Shadows help give volume to the military vest, as well as the rest of the character. But, above all, the greatest differences will be visible in the foreground. As we said in the lighting section, shadows will play an important part in separating the harpoon gun in the foreground from the character, which is much brighter, and give the image greater depth.

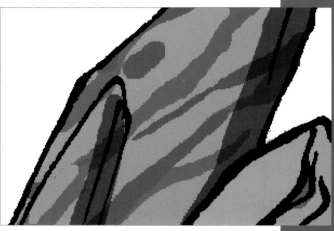

1. We'll give the vest and machete sheath a camouflage treatment.

2. This texture is achieved by adding various tones of the same color, so they form patches of color, but always fitting in with the shadows we've marked.

3. In order to draw a simple background with flat shapes, the first thing we must do is draw a color sketch where we'll arrange the main planes.

4. Now we'll use almost geometrical brush-strokes to give volume to the elements we sketched previously. We've chosen darker, more intense colors, for the foreground, and brighter and lighter colors for the background, which is where some of the light comes from.

5. Finally, we've painted a target circle as if we were looking at the jungle through a sight. The most important thing is that we use the diagonal of the cross to exaggerate the image's composition.

Finishing Touches

We'll paint the lines of the smoke from the gun being fired to give it a more ethereal look. Now we've reached the moment to put it all together. After some slight lighting adjustments, we'll go over all the elements we've used to give the image greater action. In particular, the diagonal lines and the character's inclined position, as both serve to mark movement, followed by our use of light to create depth, differentiating the foreground from the background.

SPORTS

Baseball

Tennis

Soccer

Beach Volleyball

Martial Arts

Baseball

Baseball, which was first introduced to Japan by Horace Wilson in 1872, is currently one of the most popular sports in Japan. Yet it only caught on as a mainstream success shortly after World war II, when American culture flooded Japanese society, reaching into every corner of the country. Certainly, baseball stirs a lot of passion among fans all over Japan. Its popularity is such that it plays a major role in Japanese life, which explains why you can go into any Japanese bookshop and find dozens of *manga* magazines solely dedicated to this sport. However, as a rule, you tend to find the most passionate baseball *mangas* in the *shonen* genre, aimed at younger boys. Mitsuru Adachi is probably the most prolific baseball *mangaka*, with works such as *Touch*, *H2*, *CrossGame*, and *Nine*. Other classics include *Kyoskin No Hoshi*, *3rd base 4th*, and *Miracle Giants Domu-kun*.

Shape

Let's sketch a two-character composition that captures the culminating moment between the pitcher and batter. We'll freeze it just when tension is at its highest, as the batter awaits the pitch. In order for the reader to see the two characters perfectly, we'll draw them from two different points of view: a front view of the pitcher, who we'll arch completely, and a side view of the hitter.

Volume

We'll use volume to define their particular movements, in order to maximize expression in the figures. We'll differentiate between the characters' anatomical and volumetric planes by making use of simple geometric figures when foreshortening. The baseball in the foreground seems even larger when compared to the pitcher in the background of the drawing.

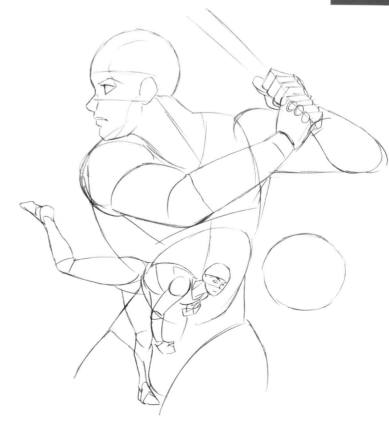

Anatomy

In this exercise, and whenever we're drawing a very dynamic action, it's necessary to put greater emphasis on the characters' movement than their anatomy. We can draw the batter's hands more easily if we first mark the position of the bat and then the hands wrapping around it, gripping it tightly. The batter's expression should portray intensity: a challenging look in his eyes, knitting his brow, with lips pursed and teeth clenched.

Final Sketch

We'll complete the drawing by adding the uniforms. We'll draw the wrinkles in their clothing by following the direction of the athletes' movements. Then we'll make sure we give the baseball its trademark seam pattern. We can always use the internet to find references when drawing accessories, such as the batter's helmet, making the scene more realistic.

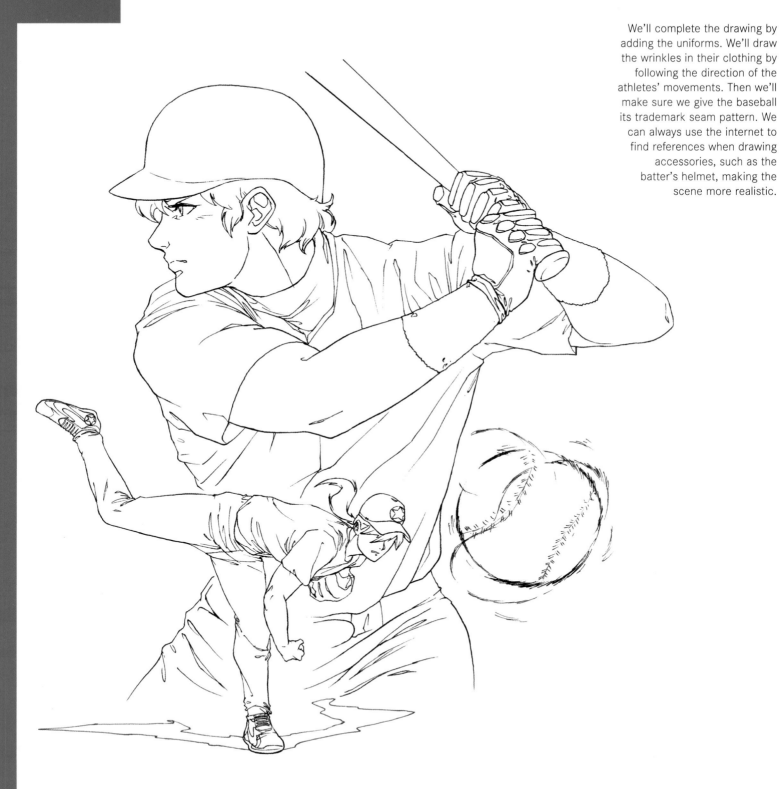

Lighting

Here we'll mark the direction of the primary light source and the shaded areas. In this case we'll be looking for contrast when drawing an intense zenithal light, which comes from somewhere above the characters. We'll save more attractive lighting tones for shinier materials. Their clothing will benefit from softer tones since its texture is more matt.

Flat Colors

We'll go on to give the illustration some color by painting the players' different team uniforms. The dark color used for the batter in the background will serve to contrast nicely with the bright red we've chosen for the pitcher. We'll shape the decorative borders by following the wrinkles we've marked in the drawing, giving the clothing greater volume.

Shading

Shading definitely does a lot to shape the characters' overall anatomy. We'll define the figures by basing them on the volumes we've previously constructed in the volume and lighting sections. We'll use white within colored objects in order to mark brighter shiny areas. The ball's shadow is broken in order to visually suggest that it is actually in movement.

1. Prepare the texts to put on the uniforms.

2. Adapt them to the direction of the clothing's fabric, and then shape the text on top of the wrinkles.

3. Finally leave only the areas of the text that are visible and then apply shading, while following the creases in the clothing.

Finishing Touches

We'll add lighting and shading tones that complement the characters' shapes, while adhering to the criteria regarding light contrast that we mentioned previously. We'll finish defining the print on the clothing by adapting it to the volumes. Then we'll go over the shaded lines in order to achieve a more ethereal consistency, differentiating them from the physical bodies. Finally, we'll give the composition a background.

Tennis

Tennis is another sport that's picking up steam in Japan. Today we can still remember the influence of *Ace o Nerea*, a serie from the 70's that, together with its animated version, reached all four corners of the world and which is still one of the most famous series within the *shojo* genre. *Ace o Nerea* brought tennis to animation's front line, and the human drama of its protagonists to the hearts of spectators. Nowadays, *The Prince of Tennis* is one of the *shonen manga* that has brought this sport back up to number one in sales. The widespread success of tennis can also be attributed to the passion Japanese people feel for all those sports where the stars take on a dimension greater than a merely athletic one. In our case we're going to be drawing a young tennis player who could just as well earn a living modeling bathing suits. A good example for girls, and one much desired by boys.

Shape

When shaping the girls it's a good idea to remember their hourglass shape. In other words, we have to draw nice hips that create an attractive feminine figure. We'll shape her movement positioning for a backhand, so the arm holding the racquet overlaps a good part of her body. Even so, it's a good idea to sketch the areas that won't be visible in the end.

Volume

When working volumes we must strengthen and elongate the athlete's body.
By slightly lowering the point of view we'll manage to stylize the girl's legs even more, even if as it is we've already drawn them to look quite long. Stylizing figures is a very common tool used in *manga*, especially in areas of the body such as the legs.

Anatomy

It's a good idea to use smooth, rounded shapes when detailing the female anatomy of an attractive girl like this. We can define some of her muscles, such as the outline of her arms and legs, giving her the kind of muscle tone we expect from athletes. We'll finish her face by adding smooth, rounded features, but with a look that suggests great determination and strength.

Final sketch

We'll dress the character up in a simple tennis outfit. We can play with raising her miniskirt to show a bit of her panties. We can also add wristbands, visors or hats and, of course, sports shoes. We'll finish by drawing the racquet and ball, which we'll give a typical hair-like structure by drawing broken lines that are different from those of the rest of the drawing.

Lighting

As whenever we're working with lighting, we won't limit ourselves to shaping the figures, we'll also be working the texture of each object. In this case there are three different types of lines: rounded ones for her body, more angular ones for the clothing fabric and finally, a broken one for the material of the ball, the wristbands and the band around the visor.

Flat Colors

This is going to be very simple. In order to achieve the prototypical Caucasian girl we'll paint her hair yellow and her eyes, light blue. It's also a good idea to paint her skin a light color. Tennis outfits are usually white, but we'll contrast it with pink wristbands and her panties peeking out from below her uplifted clothes. We can design a logotype for her racquet and incorporate it later with woven strings.

Shading

We'll draw the tennis player's skin so that it looks shiny and sweaty. We can achieve this effect by using a third, more intense color or shade when sectioning color, and by painting highlights on the lighted areas. We can also resort to this effect when we wish to create more angular shadows on her dress.

1. For her racquet we'll use a web of squares which we'll incline over the surface where we've drawn the logotype.

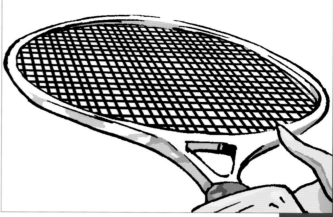

2. Draw the netting so that the lines (in this case the vertical ones) run towards the same point on the horizon.

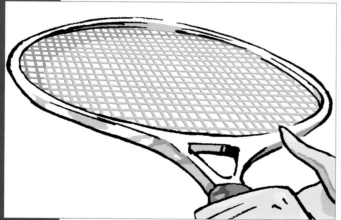

3. Finally color it, if possible using the same range of colors that we used in her outfit.

4. In order to create the background effect, we'll directly paint the stands that can be seen behind the tennis player. Afterwards we'll blur them so they remain in the background.

Finishing Touches

We'll finish the illustration by scraping the background as if with a stone in order to create a rough scratchy texture. This effect helps put it even further away. It also evokes the clay surfaces of some tennis courts. Finally, we'll project the tennis player's shadow over the surface she's standing on.

Soccer

For many years baseball was Japan's national sport. In fact, it still is today. But the popularity of their national team has helped soccer grow in the land of the Rising Sun. In recent years, great soccer stars have left their mark in Japan as trainers or even finishing their careers in the Japanese soccer league. The media's coverage of the 2002 World Cup held in Japan and Korea gave the sport a tremendous boost, and today the Japanese are just as interested in soccer as they are in baseball.

In *manga* we can find an overwhelming number of series that are dedicated to the sport, some of them are internationally famous such as *Captain Tsubasa* by Yoichi Takahashi which first came out in 1981 in the magazine *Shonen Jump*. Once again, *anime* adaptations of *Tsubasa* and other series like *Aoki Densetsu Shoot!*, *Fight!*, *Kickers*, *Whistle!*, *Hungry Heart Wild Striker* and *Ashita e Free Kick* have taken soccer all the way to the forefront in *mangas*.

Shape

If we want to capture the excitement of a given sport in a single image, it's important to learn to pick the right moment. In soccer it's typical to choose the moment the ball is being kicked towards the goal, or some other spectacular action. We've opted for a moment where a player is dribbling and feinting around another. This way we'll be working with two figures located in the same space and horizon, on the same part of the field.

Volume

It's a good idea to choose a low point of view, near the ground, when drawing soccer scenes, since it brings the viewer's eye closer to the center of the action: the ball. By lowering the point of view, all volumes should be drawn somewhat foreshortened, slightly smaller as we go up towards their heads. Their legs are important and placing their feet properly is an absolute must.

Anatomy

Athletes have strong, agile, well-shaped bodies. When we look at soccer players we can see their legs are built with powerful muscles, since that's where their strength is concentrated. Their arms swing in time with their running, and often they are drawn more loosely, with wide arcs crossing their chest. Their hair flies behind them as they're running.

Final Sketch

Our character's eyes can be looking up, with decision, as if concentrating on his final objective: the goal. As far as his clothes are concerned, the most important thing is to represent the tension in the wrinkles. The cleats are very special as well, so it's a good idea to be familiar with them in order to draw them correctly. We'll blur the details of the ball in order to show it moving.

Lighting

By using zenithal lighting we'll naturally shape the shadows on the athletes. In addition to marking the main volumes, working with shading also helps to highlight their muscles. We'll also have to define the way their movement affects the wrinkles in their clothes. The projected shadows define the area of the field the players are running on.

Flat Colors

In the first place, we'll have to differentiate the players' uniforms. It's important to use different colors and, if possible, to even use opposite colors to exaggerate the difference even more. We can be creative, as we've done here with the second player, and design a uniform that combines shapes and colors. We can differentiate the two players even more by also making their skin and hair color different.

Shading

At this stage we'll be differentiating the textures of each of the elements in the drawing. In other words, the soft, rounded lines used in drawing their skin will be different from the more angular lines used in their clothes and the broken lines used to exaggerate the ball in movement. Tonal difference will also become evident in shinier areas such as their hair.

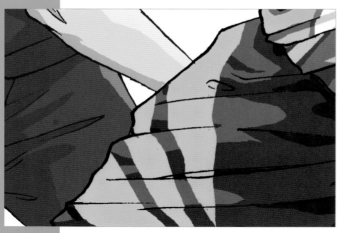

1. Draw the pattern on the uniform by following the wrinkles so they fit the volumes of the clothes.

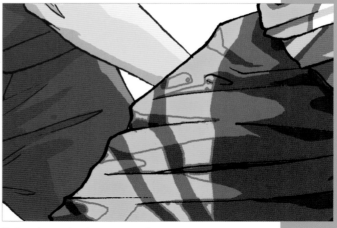

2. Continue shaping the shading on the new pattern just as we did on his shorts.

3. Finish filling in the shaded areas with the corresponding color (depending on the one used in the pattern).

4. Give the shadow greater depth by lightening the area that's furthest from the viewer.

Finishing Touches

Adding lighter areas to the character's skin will make it look shiny with sweat and effort. We'll finish the uniforms by adding whatever details we deem necessary to enrich the drawing, always making sure to respect volume and lighting. Lastly, we've added a small area of sky which will give our composition some movement thanks to its spiral shape.

Beach Volleyball

The beach is one of the best places to play sports. It's very common to find *manga* and *anime* series that place some of their stories in this environment due to the characteristics associated with it: it's a place for vacations, for relaxing, for fun, for summer romances... Lots of activities can take place on the beach, but we'll just focus on those related to sports. In this illustration we'll connect a ball sport with a martial art. On the one hand we have the attractive volleyball girls, and on the other the acrobatic boys practicing *capoeira*. To do this we'll combine different planes with a daring layout seen from a low point-of-view with a forced perspective. This type of setting helps us create dynamic compositions and emphasizes the characters' actions.

We'll use this illustration as a transition to the section on disciplined martial arts, which are the stars of an enormous amount of *manga* and *anime* series.

Shape

For this exercise we'll be drawing lots of figures on the sand, in various positions and with different ways of holding themselves up. Whenever we do this we should be very careful not to lose the reference of our floor. In this illustration we've drawn the horizon line at sea level. This will help us not to lose track of our relation to space and to respect our characters' proportions.

Volume

Paying attention to the perspective we've marked when shaping, we'll draw the volumes over which we'll construct the characters. These must be drawn according to the perspective, with the corresponding foreshortening, especially the characters' leg in the foreground. This way we'll highlight the low point-of-view we've chosen for this setting. The upper parts of the characters will look smaller.

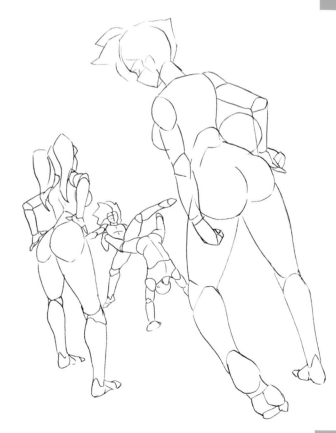

Anatomy

Without a doubt, in this drawing the svelte bodies of the girls in the foreground are meant to grab the reader's attention. This makes it especially important that we draw their anatomies correctly, and that they look attractive. We can exaggerate female attributes such as their breasts and hips, since this is another of the more common tricks used in manga. The bodies of the boys also present an anatomy that reflects hours spent at the gym.

Final Sketch

We'll complete our illustration by drawing their clothes. In this case they're not wearing very much, but we can still carefully study how wrinkles form with tension. They form whenever something pulls at a piece of clothing. These creases should be drawn with direct and energetic strokes towards the point where the tension originates as we can see on the girls' clothes and around the knee of the pants of the boy who's kicking the ball.

Lighting

Whenever we are drawing an outdoor scene with intense light we should remember that our shadows should show a lot of contrast. This will also make it so the shadow contours will be very clearly defined. The projected shadows will also help us understand volume better and the proper position of objects, such as the hand of the girl with pigtails, who is projecting a shadow over her hips.

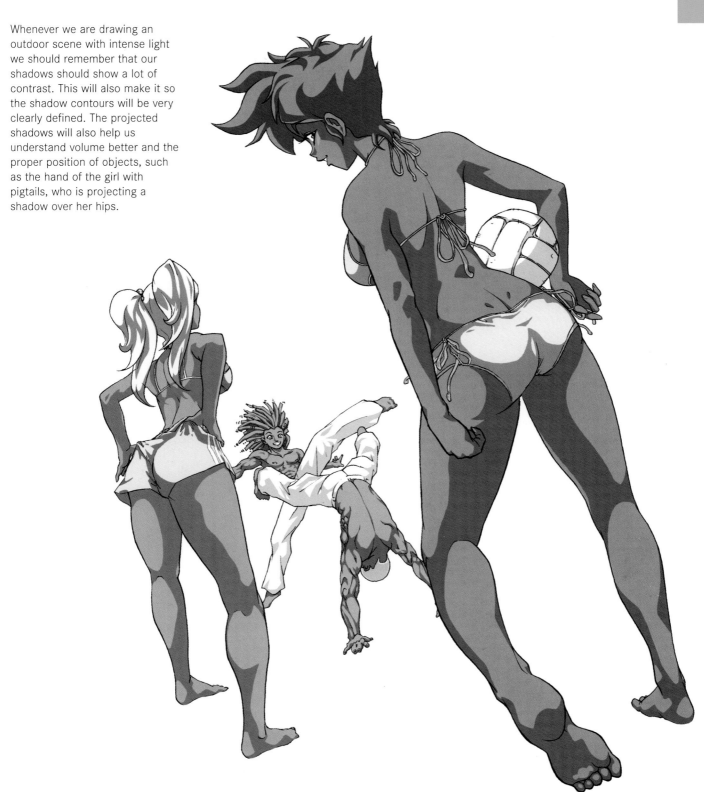

Flat Colors

It's always better to select a warm and bright color palette for this kind of situation. We can also work with light colors that are quite saturated in order to portray the brightness of the moment. By doing this we manage to transmit the atmosphere of a hot, sunny day at the beach. We'll choose green and blue for the colors of their bikinis, which will contrast with the range of oranges and browns used on their tanned bodies.

Shading

We'll move ahead and shape the shadows just as we mentioned in the lighting section. We can go over the shadow contours, adding bright highlights to their skin so it looks shiny and tanned. The text we've added on the bathing suit has been drawn to adapt to the wrinkles of the fabric, thus accentuating its volume.

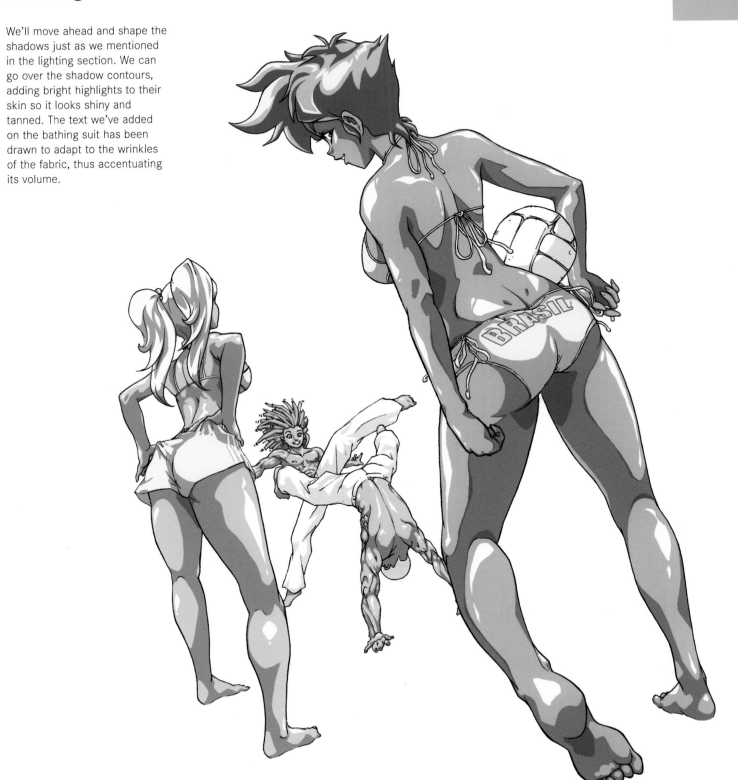

1. We'll begin by making a sketch when drawing the background. Its colors should match those of the rest of the illustration.

2. Next we'll draw the final part, detailing the background elements.

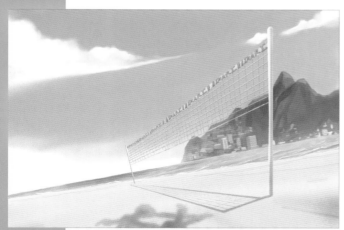

3. We'll finish by adding all the little details, like the text on the net, the sand, projected shadows of the characters.

4. Elements that are furthest away should be drawn to look a bit hazy and blue on account of the aerial perspective. We can add some grain to achieve the sandy texture, and smooth white brushstrokes will give us the shape of the crests of the waves breaking in the distance.

Finishing Touches

Lastly, we'll put our characters and background together to form our final illustration. Working each element separately gives us greater freedom when it comes to painting and coloring techniques, but it's crucial that we respect our color palette, lighting and tone. By combining flat colors for the characters and picturesque backgrounds we achieve a pretty and pleasing *anime*.

Martial Arts

Martial arts are fighting arts whose techniques are organized around coherent systems that must be studied for many years. They involve practicing set movements which often include deep spiritual and philosophical dimensions. Rather than being a path towards violence, martial arts are a path towards self-awareness and personal achievement. Some of the most famous martial arts come from Japan. Those that came about before the Meiji Restoration (1868) are called *koryu budo*. This category groups together a wide variety of schools and styles, many of which are related to the ancient arts of *ninjitsu* and *kenjutsu* (art of the sword). The term *gendai budo* refers to new martial arts that emerged after the Restoration such as *judo*, *kendo* and *aikido*. The roots of *sumo* go back over a thousand years, and its origin in Japan is connected with religion and mythology.

Shape

Whenever we create a composition with various characters, shaping becomes the most important aspect of the illustration. We should sketch all the figures we want to appear in the final drawing in order to determine their position and proportion, thus controlling all points of interest and the order in which the image will be read, which is usually clockwise.

Volume

At this stage we'll define each character's volume and determine how much space we're going to give each figure. It's time to begin defining the characters' personalities, whether masculine or feminine. We will also determine the type of shaping required depending on their body types, which can be more or less voluminous or stylized.

Anatomy

It is highly important to develop character, making sure we give each figure its own personality. The *sumo* wrestler will be enormous and well-concentrated. If we draw a thin *judoka* her gesture should be determined and body agile in order to face up to heavier fighters. We'll also develop the determination of the *kendo* fighter and the *karateka's* strength.

Final Sketch

It's time to gather together our references. Each of the martial arts has its own unique and specific outfit. It's important to know what kind of clothes each fighter should be wearing, since it generally forms part of the concept of each discipline and is the fruit of a long tradition. Not to mention also in disciplines like *kendo* they wear protection and use a weapon known as a *shinai*.

Lighting

In these kinds of compositions it's not necessary for all the characters to be highlighted in the same way. In fact, lighting can be used as another method of visually separating the figures, and giving each of them their own space. In this case all of the characters have similar highlighting, but none of them projects shadows over any of the others, since the intention is for them to all be separate.

Flat Colors

In martial arts colors usually take on a significance that goes well beyond the obvious. In *judo* the color of the belt tells us the rank of the *judoka* wearing it. In *sumo*, the color of the *mawashi* (the belt the *rikiski* or wrestler wears) is also important. Gathering references is a way of gaining knowledge and certainly helps enrich our illustrations.

Shading

At this stage we'll be giving our characters some more shape. We've given each of them a different skin color to make their differences even more apparent. The clothing worn by the *karateka* and the *judoka* can make them look very similar, and even confuse the readers, so that's why it's important to differentiate the two as much as possible.

1. In order to mark folds in a piece of clothing that wrinkles, we can outline the border with shading of a darker color.

2. We can draw the *kendo* fighter's armor using colors with different contrasts in their flatness, lighting and shading in order to differentiate the different textures. The fabrics are more matt and the breastplate slightly shinier.

3. Since we've only chosen Japanese martial arts, we'll use the Japanese flag as a background. Besides, the circle will help us close the composition.

Finishing Touches

We've finished the job by adding some final adjustments to the characters' shading and lighting. The red in the Japanese flag can add something extra to any illustration featuring Japanese martial arts: the force and passion of blood and the sun. All illustrators should try mastering the use of different colors to awaken feelings in the reader.

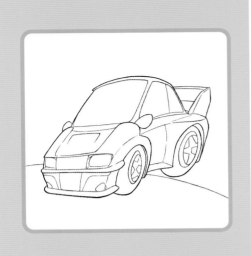

MECHA AND VEHICLES

SD Car

Fighter Plane

SD Robot

Giant Robot

Robot Pilot

Combat Armor

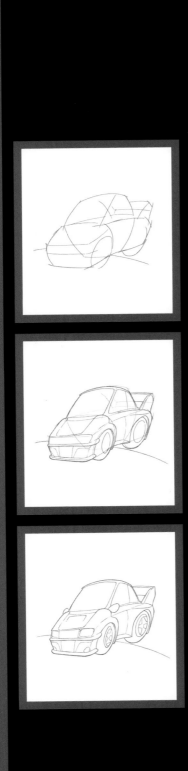

SD car

Not even vehicles can manage to escape being targeted as *super-deformed* parodies; in fact, this phenomenon has even inspired videogame sagas in Japan. In this illustration we're going to seek inspiration in two classic trend-setting references.

The first of which is the legendary Sega videogame *Out Run*, which has gone on to inspire hundreds of other games since its release in 1986, with its characteristic beach atmosphere and logotype. You could say the relationship between *manga* and videogames has been a very productive one.

Our second reference is *Choro Q* cars. These vehicles came out in 1978 and have managed to stay at the forefront ever since. They are known for the caricatures of the models they were based on. They've actually become so famous in Japan that life-size versions have been sold on the market, all set to drive around the city. It's perfectly common to find hundreds of these designs in *mangas*, particularly in those of a more humorous nature.

Shape

Whenever we draw a vehicle, especially a car, we can stick to a basic foolproof scheme. In this case we're going to draw three volumes almost as if they were elliptical spheres, or rounded cubes. Each of them will be related to one of the three basic parts of a conventional car: motor, interior, trunk. With this foundation we can go about reproducing just about any car.

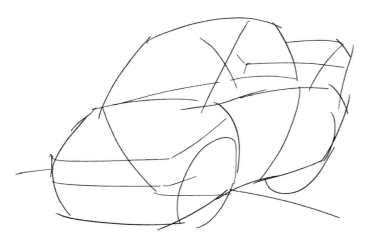

Volume

When drawing vehicles we see that their structure is almost completely defined by their volume. Whenever we're drawing rigid, inorganic objects it's a good idea to use rulers and stencil curves which will help us achieve a colder look. In this particular case the curved lines will define the vehicle's character since we are caricaturing its look.

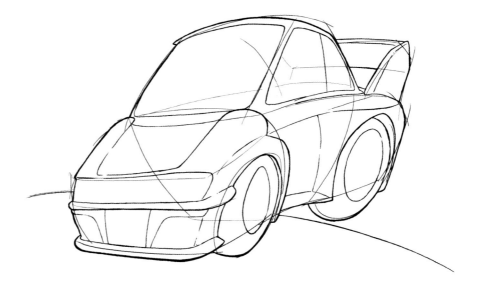

Anatomy

In this section we'll focus on the vehicle's more characteristic details. It's time to draw the headlights, mud flaps, rearview mirrors, rims, etc. We mustn't forget we are dealing with an SD version and that this means we can exaggerate the proportions of the interior with flattened shapes on the ends, giant wheels and a certain deformation of its structure.

Final Sketch

Let's finish the drawing with a background that matches our illustration. We'll caricature the background elements by synthesizing shapes. We'll use simple, rounded shapes for the road and mountains. Vegetation, such as the palm trees, can be drawn with less detail, focusing on their silhouettes. We can simulate perspective by drawing different mountain planes.

Lighting

Lighting will also be treated in a simple manner. When drawing vehicles, or any metallic object, we usually use tones that are quite different from each other, since the greater the contrast, the more an object's texture will shine. The extreme is the chrome elements, such as in this illustration, where we find the most contrast in the car's glass windows.

Flat Colors

It's a good idea to choose bright, contrasting colors. In this case we'll choose red for our car. The color red is connected with luxury sports cars and powerful cars. But it's also a perfect color to contrast with the background we've chosen, where green predominates. Red and green are complementary colors, assuring that we achieve maximum contrast between the figure and its background.

Shading

We'll shape all the objects with the corresponding color of shade. When we work with shading we're not only working with the object's lighting but we're also giving it texture. We'll use stripes and dots for the palm tree's trunk, and combine short, loose, quick strokes for the grass. The vehicle's shape has a lot of sections, imitating the metallic effect, while the road is covered with smooth dots to resemble gravel.

1. Place the car's logotypes by paying careful attention to the inclination of the car's bodywork, as the blue squares indicate.

2. Paint the lines in the background black to create a picturesque effect that separates it from the foreground.

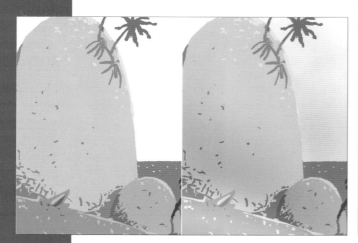

3. We can softly fade color to complement the illustration's shape, saturating the elements and making them bright.

4. Finish by creating a clipping mask for the final step.

Finishing Touches

The illustration's finish should look something like a promotional logotype. We've achieved this by creating a clipping mask that will serve to give the entire drawing shape, unifying the visual image. This way of working with color was very common in the early days of video-game illustration and it still influences lots of graphic artwork today.

Fighter Plane

Combat airplanes are among the most attractive vehicles and have been fantasized about in all kinds of action and adventure stories. *Manga* is clearly no exception. Hundreds of different airplanes, real and imaginary, have become protagonists of all sorts of action and adventure stories. From Kaoru Shintai's legendary work *Area 88*, which inspired animation series and videogames with its war deeds and spectacular aerial battles, to *Macross*, the work of Shoji Kawamori that revolutionized the world of *space operas* with its *Valkyrias*, fighter planes capable of transforming into gigantic robots. It goes without saying every true-blue space saga has its characteristic aircraft, rapid machines with tremendous fire-power capacity and overwhelming maneuverability, capable of destroying an entire enemy fleet. This premise has inspired hundreds of videogames with legions of followers in Japan. It's the genre referred to as *shooters*.

Shape

As we saw earlier with the car exercise and, generally speaking, whenever we have to draw any kind of vehicle, it's a good idea for us to begin by shaping the areas we think are essential for our machine: cabin, motor, wings and aerodynamic devices (if this is designed to be maneuvered within the atmosphere and not in outer space), etc.

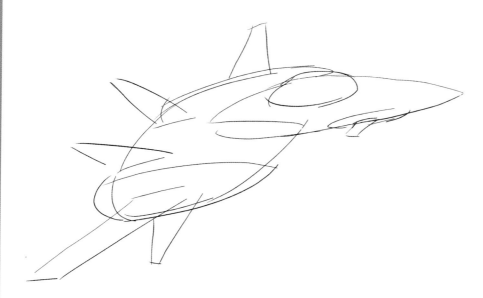

Volume

The volume stage is usually crucial. For this it's a good idea to collect as many references as we can to help us create the type of vehicle we're looking for. We can also, collect separate ideas and make them into something totally different as if we were making a collage. It's a good idea to first use simple shapes to make the use of perspective easier.

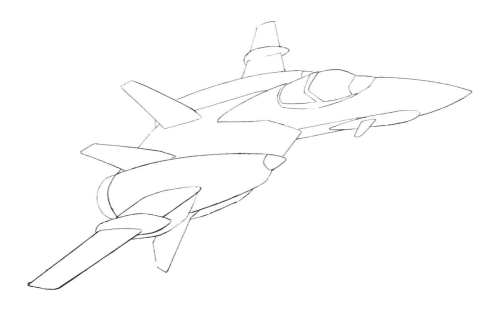

Anatomy

Now we'll move on to draw the finer details of our aircraft. In this case we begin by using a base of a real combat fighter, although in reality it's made of fragments of different airplanes to which we've added much bigger motors. Sometimes the simplest ideas manage to convey the most: bigger motors will make the plane go further and move quicker.

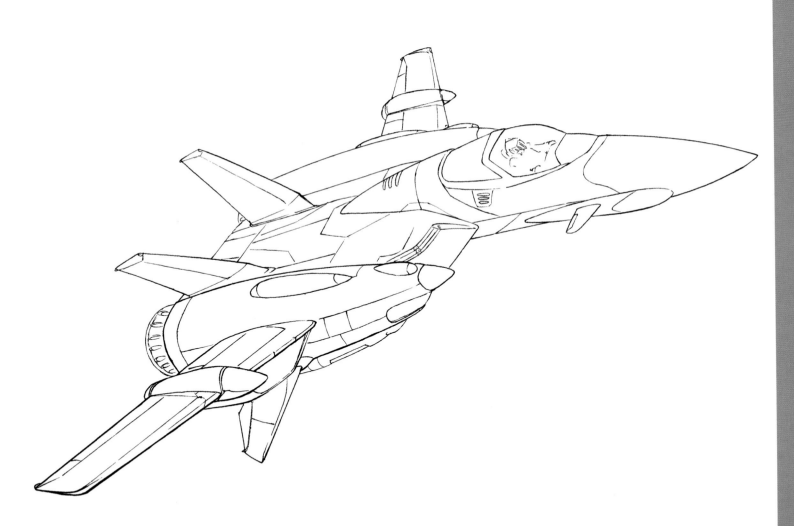

Final Sketch

Now is the time for resourcefulness. We've added lots of details that will make the aircraft look more realistic- or at least it will appear so by the way the details have been drawn. Whenever we invent vehicles or mechanical elements, it's a good idea to try to imagine that these must be able to function in the real world. This will help us draw them more realistically. Our final detail is the particle cannon that the ship holds in the lower part of its fuselage.

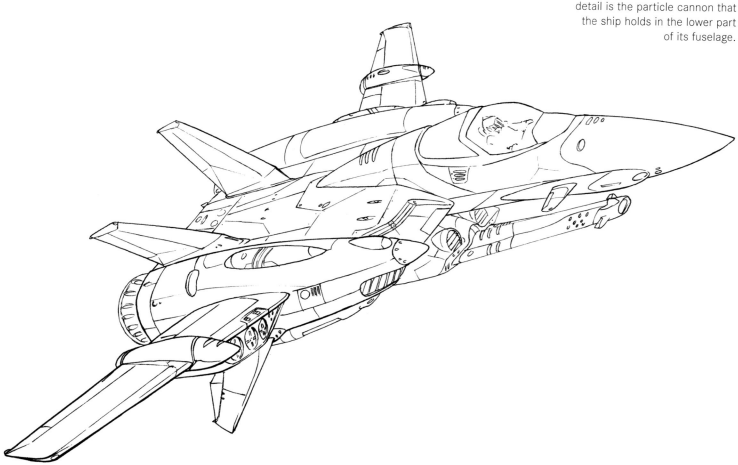

Lighting

Whenever we want to create a special lighting effect in the background of an illustration, we should first think how this might affect the figures. In this case we're going to get them ready to be seen against the light, with the sun in the background. We'll have lots of shadows all throughout the drawing, leaving the lighting in second position. The projected shadows will be very hard.

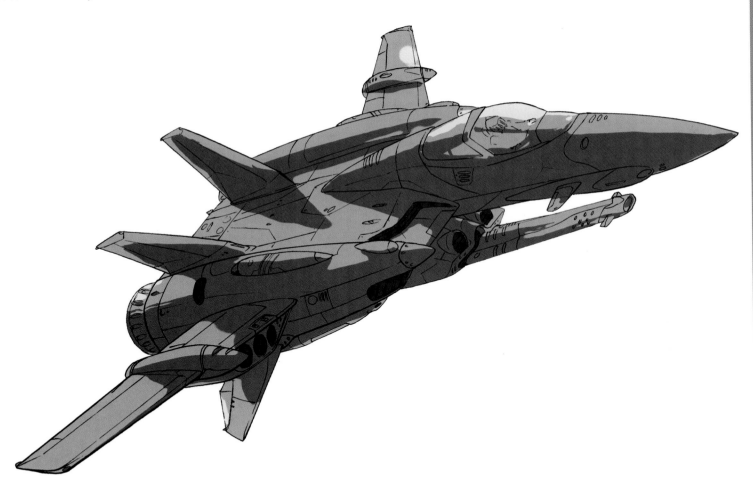

Flat Colors

As we already explained in some of the other exercises, because of their symbolic power, colors are fundamental in order for the reader to identify the characters and the main elements of a story. Vehicles should reflect a pilot's personality. In this case we've chosen the color orange and some shapes that recall our studio's logotype.

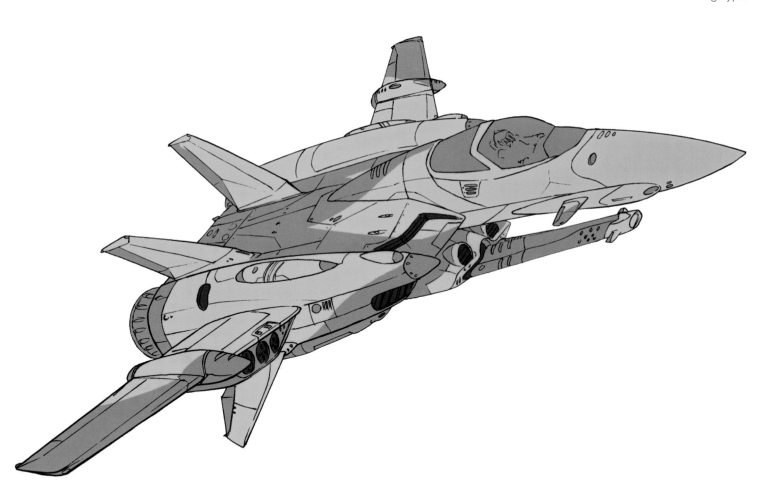

Shading

On account of the lighting we've chosen for this illustration, there will be a lot of contrast between the colors used for shading and lighting. The color sections don't have edges and color is worked in order to accentuate the smooth texture of metal. We'll find the shiniest colors in the cabin, thanks to the use of glass.

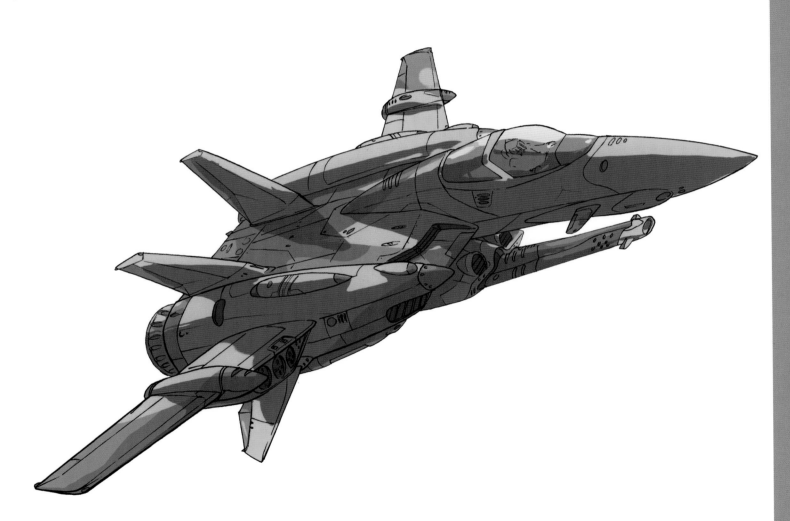

Tips and Tricks

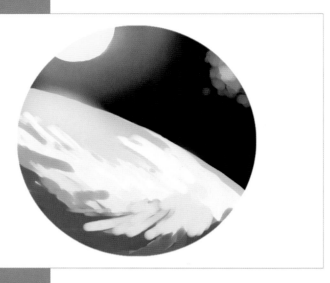

1. Let's paint a special space background with a sun creating a view against the light. The first thing we should do is spread color over the areas we're going to be painting, thinking about how to position each element in the image.

2. We'll begin shaping the color with shorter brushstrokes. In all the lighting areas we'll make sure we mix part of the yellow coming from the main light source. We'll smooth the textures of the clouds and shape the horizon.

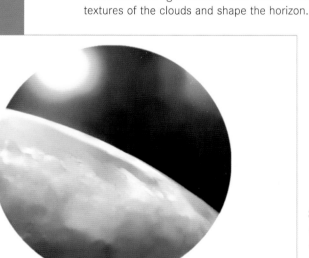

3. We'll finish by cleaning and fading the color of the sun so it looks really bright. The crests of the clouds should have the roughest texture in the image. We'll add stars by using small points of color over the black of the space and the blue of the clouds.

Finishing Touches

We'll integrate the fighter-plane will the background we just finished drawing and add small touches of light over the areas of the plane that are exposed to the sun. We can paint small highlights on the highest parts of the vehicle's curves: these will help give the machine volume. Looking at our composition we can see an "X" shape between the direction of the fighter plane and the outline of the planet. This arrangement gives this snapshot some movement.

SD Robot

It's difficult to know if the love the Japanese share for robots stems from *manga* or if *manga* is just a reflection of it. What's for sure is that robots are one of the most popular topics in both children's and adult *manga*. The myth of the iron man has been interpreted hundreds of times in all sorts of *manga* genres to varying degrees of success, although generally quite spectacular. In fact, in the West it is considered the *manga* genre par excellence. And as with any other famous genre, robots have also had the luxury of being parodied. Many generations of Japanese have enjoyed *anime* and *manga* series as well as videogames where the kind and big-headed brothers of their favorite giant robots confronted hilarious versions of their most bitter enemies. The robot genre also happens to be where the super-deformed have made their greatest presence. A lot kinder, but just as fantastic and powerful, SD's often become firm favorites.

Shape

Small size and fun proportions don't usually take away from the dynamism of these SD robots. We'll take advantage of this and choose a dynamic action position. Whenever we want to show a character about to enter combat it's important to pay attention to the lean of their body. When we incline the body forwards we show they are anxious to enter into the action. The positioning of the feet should also be very dynamic.

Volume

Generally speaking, *super-deformed* versions of gigantic robots tend to be a lot simpler and less baroque than their originals. With SD proportions we'll sketch simple volumes for the mechanical parts of the torso and extremities. We'll draw the cranium as if it were a helmet. The lack of hair is evident, but you'll usually find other elements such as visors, horns, antennas, etc.

1. To develop volumes use our initial shape drawing as our base.

2. Begin from the back to the front, drawing simple geometric shapes.

3. Overlap volumes which are nearer the front.

4. Draw complete shapes, even when dealing with non-visible areas.

5. When drawing the front of a foreshortened part, increase the size according to perspective.

6. Finally, define the visible parts of the foreshortened arm.

Anatomy

Evidently, the robot doesn't have a human body per se, although we've based our drawing on armor. Mechanical components are always more geometrical than human body parts. And despite being an SD, in order to transmit the sensation that we are dealing with an inorganic object, we should make sure soft and rounded shapes also contain more angular areas.

Final Sketch

We'll finish the drawing adding all sorts of details which complement the robot's mechanics. We'll work on the joints and divide the units comprising each articulation. We can add some nozzles, weapons, wings and gemstones to the different areas of the robot. The lines shaping the character grow in accordance with the foreshortened areas in order to represent closer elements such as its hand or leg.

Lighting

Robots are basically built of metallic mechanical parts. This explains why, depending on the type of lighting chosen, sharp contrast in the tones is used in each area. Highlights imitating chrome parts are ever-present in these kinds of characters, and they're quite easy to achieve if we divide the color areas into sections.

Flat Colors

A robot's color is often related to its personality. Light colors tend to be chosen for robots with a kinder disposition, while dark colors are more often used to depict more aggressive robots. Bright, eye-catching colors are today's trend, especially among leading protagonist robots. We've decided to color our SD robot using a white base, along with red, yellow and blue.

Shading

We'll shape the character's volume with color but it's necessary to choose the correct color for the shading. Since we're painting metallic objects, not only will we darken the color noticeably, but we'll also saturate the colors considerably in order to achieve the desired metallic texture. The shapes of the chrome areas are also very characteristic, with lots of undulations and separations.

Finishing Touches

Now it's time to add highlights to the areas where light is strongest and adjust the final contrast tones when shading. We'll saturate the colors of the shadows. Our tendency when adjusting the lighting, however, will be towards pure white, achieving maximum contrast on the shiny surfaces. Once again, the projected shadow helps us define the floor our character is standing on.

Giant Robot

The word *mecha* originally comes from *meka*, the Japanese abbreviation of the English word "mechanical". In Japanese this word is used for any mechanical figure or vehicle. However, today giant robots are undoubtedly the most famous types of *mecha*. Perhaps that's why over time the term *mecha* has wound up being specifically used to refer to these mechanical giants.

The origin of the genre can be found in series like *Tetsujin 28*, also known as *IronMan 28*. This serie by Mitsuteru Yokoyama was the precursor to the giant robot genre. It featured a teenager who controlled a giant robot with a remote control box. You could say the genre's other main pillar has been the work of Go Nagai. This illustrator was the creator of *Mazinger Z*, the serie that laid the foundations for the genre and which has proved to be the most influential over time. Other famous series are *Getter Robo* and *Grendizer*.

Shape

When drawing giant robots there are a great number of tricks we can use to emphasize their proportions and give the impression we are looking at a true iron giant. In the first place, we can lower the horizon to the level of the character's knees or feet. Thanks to this low-angle perspective it will look like we are really looking up at the robot from a position on the floor and it's a whole lot bigger than us.

Volume

We'll continue working the volumes, sticking with our initial idea of enlarging the figure's proportions. The robot's legs and feet should look a lot bigger than the rest of the structure, exaggerating the low-angle perspective to the max. Doing this, will make it look like these parts of its body are much closer to us than, for example, its shoulders or head.

Anatomy

Another trick we can use that produces good results is to alter proportions. When drawing robots built using human anatomy as the foundation, these can be altered by reducing the size of their neck and head so it looks like the other body parts are all the more gigantic. The forearms, torso and shoulders are usually drawn much larger than normal.

Final Sketch

After sketching the basic shapes we'll define the drawing. It's a good idea to use geometric shapes that emphasize the robot's mechanical nature. We can also add all sorts of different structures, such as cogs, sheet metal, vents, sections, joints, etc. We can finish by arming our design with weapons, flying systems and all kinds of mechanical inventions.

Lighting

Lighting effects are definitely one of the most powerful tools we should master in order to fully emphasize the mechanical nature of the robot in our illustration. The way to do this is to use contrasting shadows and adding reflections the way you would if you were dealing with conventional chrome. The maximum points of light should also be very bright.

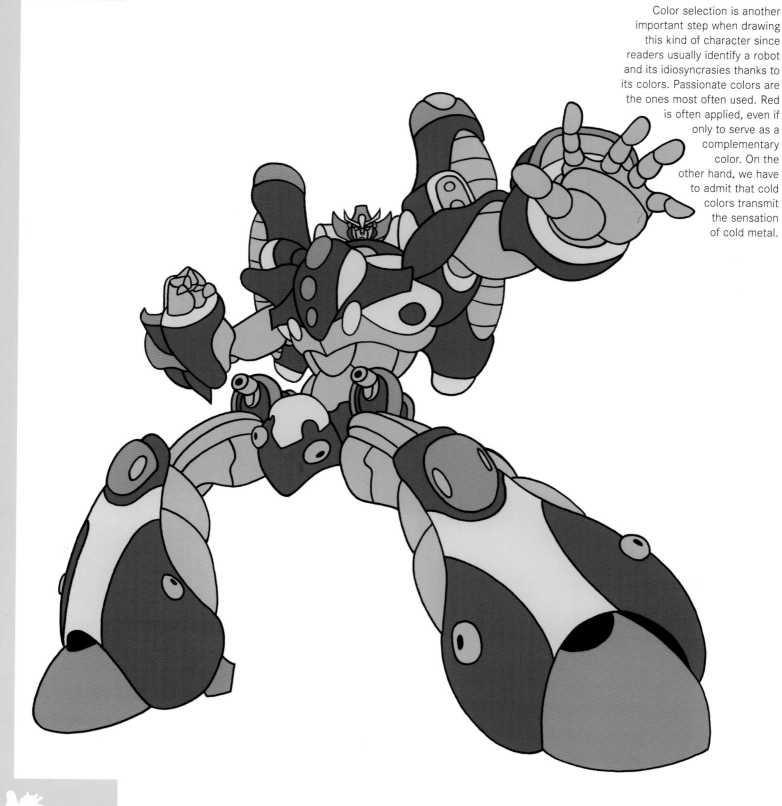

Flat Colors

Color selection is another important step when drawing this kind of character since readers usually identify a robot and its idiosyncrasies thanks to its colors. Passionate colors are the ones most often used. Red is often applied, even if only to serve as a complementary color. On the other hand, we have to admit that cold colors transmit the sensation of cold metal.

Shading

It's time to add the elements that will round out the illustration. In our case, the secret flamboyant weapon we can see in the robot's right hand. Sometimes, some elements, such as laser swords or other weapons, can serve as points of light that influence our highlighting. Afterwards we'll shape the structure as we detailed when we were studying our lighting.

Tips and Tricks

1. When painting elements such as fire and lasers it's a good idea to get rid of the border lines, in order to produce a more plasmatic, ethereal sensation.

2. After outlining the shape of the flame, we'll proceed to paint each of the different areas, selecting the colors we're going to use. We'll use white for the parts that are white-hot.

3. Finally, we can fade the flame so it looks less consistent. This way we achieve the plasmatic texture we've already mentioned. The airbrush is a great tool for achieving this.

Finishing Touches

We'll finish the illustration by adding maximum points of light in the areas of the structure that stick out the most. We'll fade the tones to further establish the metallic texture, increasing the contrast between light and shade. Then we'll add a simple background with a shape that complements the robot's position in the composition.

Robot Pilot

There's no doubt that within the *mecha* genre, robots play the leading roles. But it's also true that the soul behind a *mecha* is in fact its pilot. Hardened youngsters are in charge of getting behind the controls of these mechanical brutes, climbing inside their more or less modern, narrow cockpits. We can find as many different kinds of pilots as there are robots, but predominantly we'll find teenagers carrying the typical problems of adolescence all the way to their cockpits. Self-improvement and emotional toughness are usually put to the test, and in doing so they're actually putting a part of their souls into their robots. Piloting style is another thing to bear in mind. The most gigantic robots are usually piloted as if they were advanced combat fighters. Their little sisters, with combat armor and "mobile suits", are a lot smaller in size and are usually maneuvered using the pilot's own movements. Mental control is yet another piloting system.

Shape

The main thing we need to think about in drawing a good illustration of the robot's cockpit is choosing a good point of view that maximizes the amount of information in a single frame. We can accomplish this with distorted perspective, such as a wide-angle lens or a fish-eye lens. If we move our point of view slightly further away we can even catch a glimpse of the piloting position.

Volume

In this case we'll slightly distort the image by lowering the point of view and the horizon. Taking a shot from the pilot's left foot makes it proportionately much bigger than the rest of her body. The volumes get smaller as we move away from the point of view and emphasize perspective.

Anatomy

We've opted for a girl pilot, so in particular we should remember to accentuate her feminine curves in the areas of her breasts and hips, and to stress the hourglass shape we've already spoken about. In this case we'll shape her anatomy while we begin thinking about the cockpit's design. This way her piloting position will dictate the interior design.

Final Sketch

We can distinguish two basic types of technological finishes. If we use rough and angular shapes we'll achieve a more "retro" look, with gadgets full of levers and hundreds of buttons. On the other hand, if we choose a more ergonomic design with rounded shapes and more sober controls, we'll achieve a futuristic look such as the one seen in this illustration.

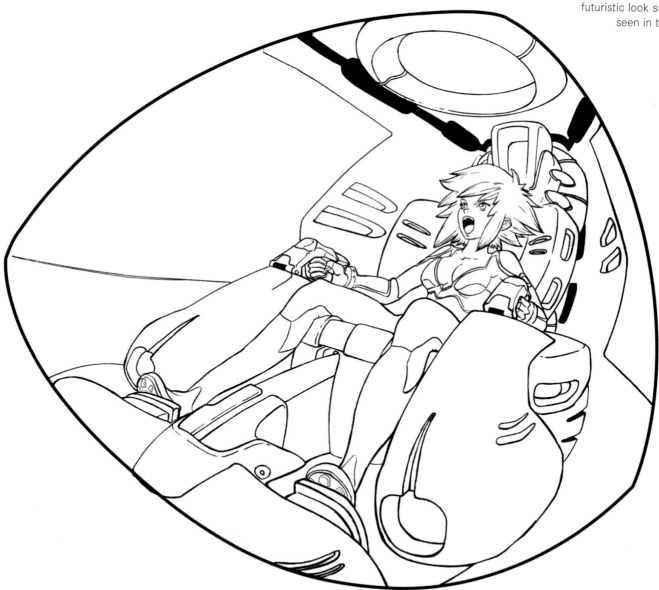

Lighting

Since we're inside a closed cockpit without windows, lighting must be totally artificial and all of it has to come from various screens and lights within the cabin. The first thing we should do is mark these points of light and clearly define the general lighting. Afterwards we'll shape the chair and the main character sitting in it.

Flat Colors

Generally speaking, we have two elements to color in. On the one hand, there's the *mecha* pilot, who usually wears a special tight and brightly-colored suit often equipped for survival in hostile environments, such as space, but which is somewhat transparent, sometimes quite overtly suggestive of the pilot's anatomy. On the other hand, we have the cabin and its much colder esthetic.

Shading

We'll shape each element in the illustration as we've done until now. The determining factor in these kinds of images is how we select the color of our shading. If, generally speaking, the tones we select should follow the colors dictated by our lighting, this becomes even more evident when it comes to shading. All of them should have the same tones: in this case, blue.

1. It's quite easy to show images on a screen and give the impression that they're totally integrated with it.

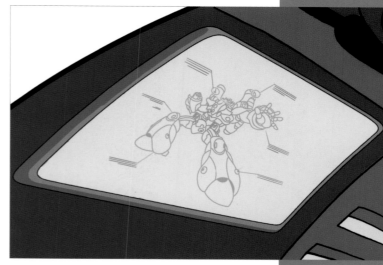

2. After defining the contours and the position of the screen, we'll superimpose the drawing we want to show, always using tones from the same range of colors as that of the screen.

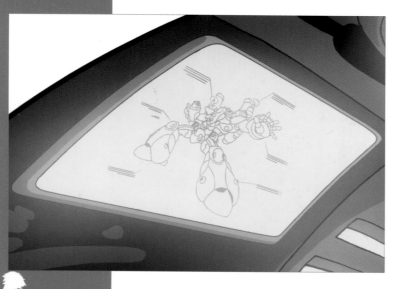

3. We'll finish by adding the kind of lighting effect screens are famous for and then our image will be fully integrated.

Finishing Touches

We'll emphasize the artificial lighting coming from the bright screens and the various points of light scattered around the cabin, spreading it across the image as if it were a veil, a soft mix of white and blue which will provide the kind of halo effect that is typical of these illustrations. This halo should also bathe the character, helping to integrate it with the scene better.

Combat Armor

Combat armor is incredibly sophisticated technology. Its main purpose is to protect those wearing it from attacks, such as enemy fire, and at the same time, provide resources and weapons, as well as communication and information systems concerning the areas they are moving about in. Without a doubt a prime example of a creator of this type of vehicle is Masamune Shirow, and the Landmates he designed for the *manga Appleseed*, which was a trendsetter in the development of these vehicles.

The armor is not driven: it responds to the movements of the person wearing it, but amplifies his strength, velocity and war capacity. The author himself says inspiration came when he saw how a mechanical exoskeleton worked. Add to that the kind of mechanical hands used in surgery and, of course, Heinlein's creations in *Starship Troopers*, a 1959 novel that explained this idea in a very clear and precise way.

Shape

In order to shape the armor in this illustration, it's necessary to also draw the person wearing it, at least whenever attempting a design for the first time. The entire structure will adapt to the user's anatomy. It's necessary that we place the joints correctly, since these will directly respond to the movements made inside.

Volume

In our particular case, we'll draw the user so he's visible, peeping out of the opening in the armor's chest piece. All the volumes should be as simple as possible so we can place the joints in their proper places. In our design we've almost only used spherical volumes. We should leave enough room for the character and the armor mechanism within the structure.

Anatomy

We can begin adding details to our powered armor. Designs are usually much smoother and more rounded than those of their gigantic robot cousins. While the latter have a tendency for fantasy, at times to the point of exaggeration or eccentricity, powered armor or landmates are usually more realistic, and heavily influenced by military style.

Final Sketch

Finally, let's get to the details. We'll continue aiming for an organic design, with simple, rounded shapes. The smooth, compact structure will give the armor a solid, robust look. The wide arms and legs will give the figure weight. We can make it look more aggressive by giving his gigantic hands some claws. In this case the weapon is a Walther PPK gun and a Vulcan machine-gun cannon. Opposites attract.

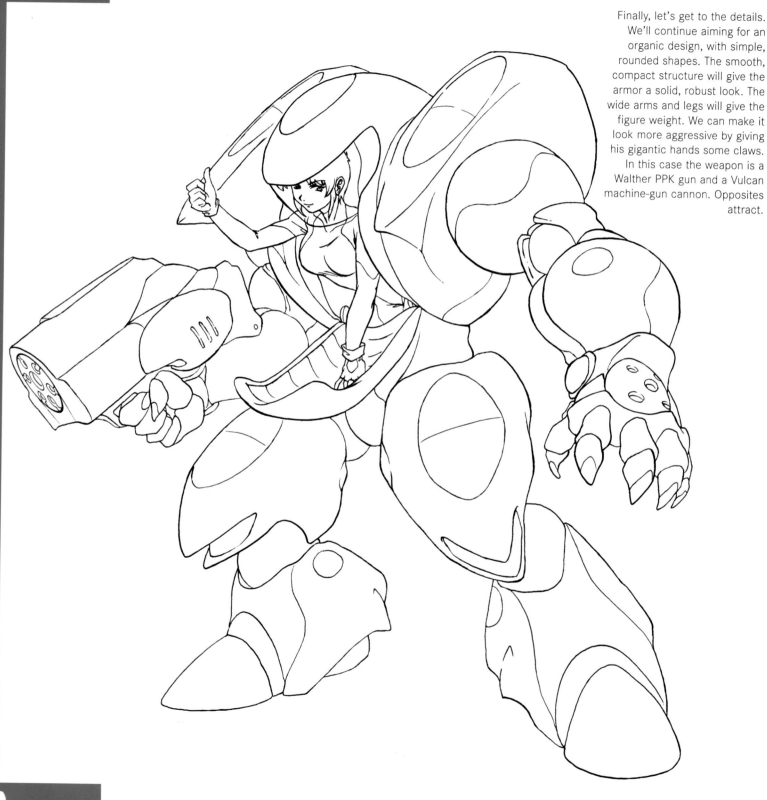

Lighting

Once again we'll take advantage of the lighting stage to refer to texture. The bulk of the image will consist of metallic materials. Even so, we can still differentiate textures. We'll draw more simple shading on matt surfaces and more complex color sections and reflections from brighter areas. Once again, projected shadows help to express volume.

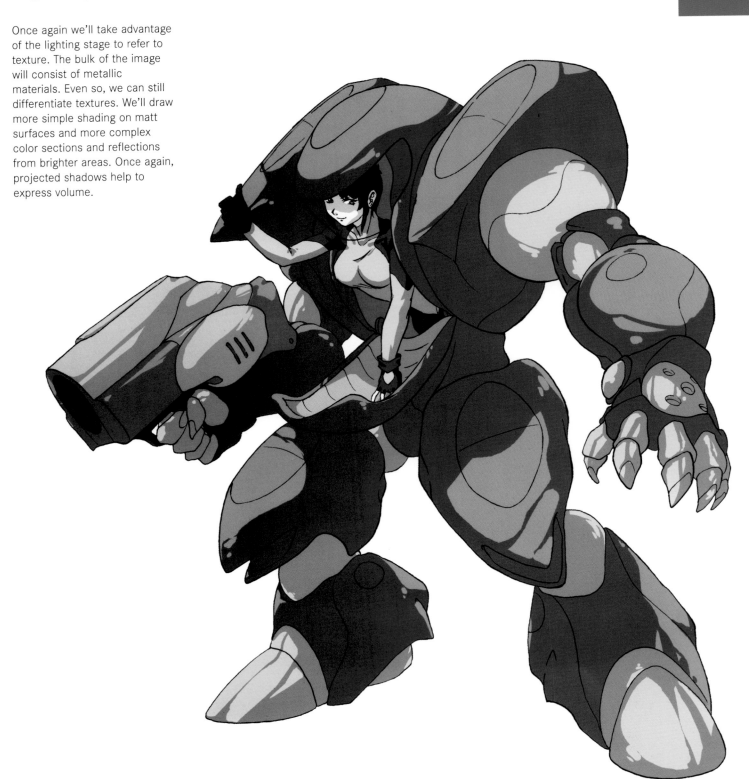

Flat Colors

There's no written rule for selecting the colors of armor. In fact, if we look at comics we can find a great range of ideas and concepts. However, it's typical to use a range of colors related to the military, such as those used in camouflage: usually, dark, cold colors tend to be chosen over brighter colors.

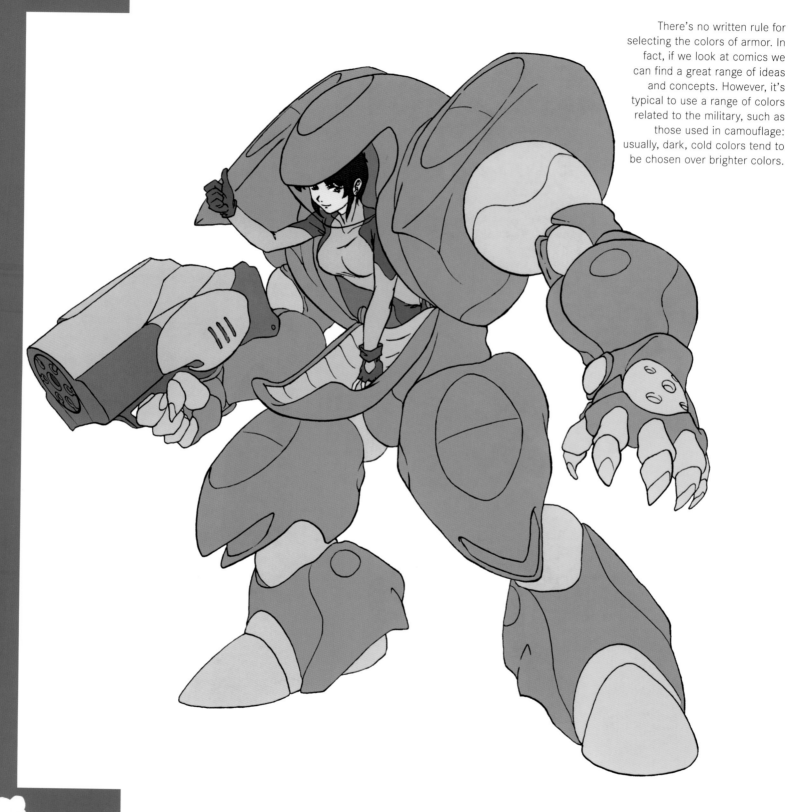

Shading

We'll paint our armor dark
green, but we'll keep some of its
original metallic color. In doing
this we assure ourselves that
the reader will unconsciously
associate the characteristics of
metal with the entire structure.
We'll use magenta for the visor
and other details, since this
color goes well with the green
we've chosen.

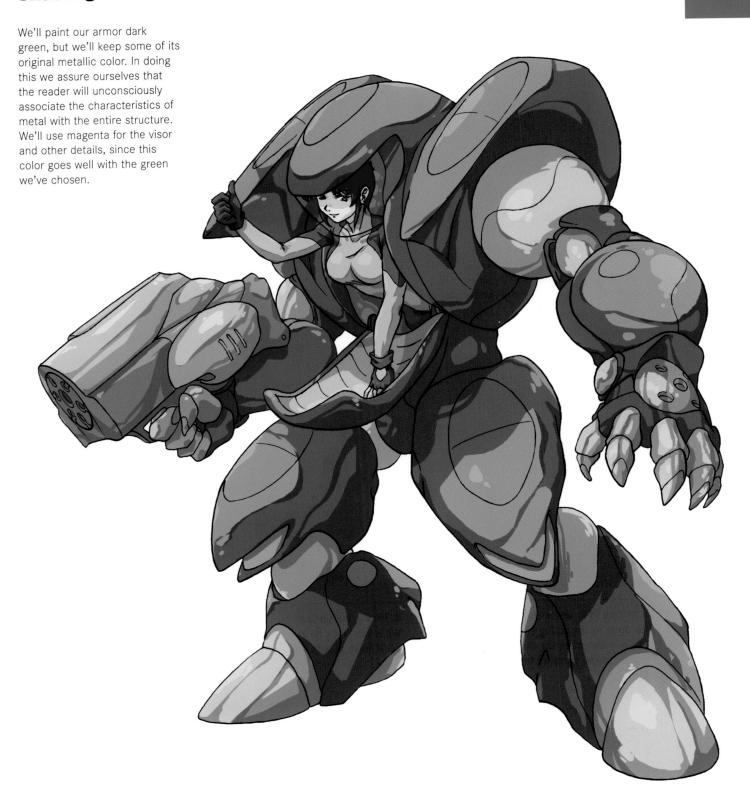

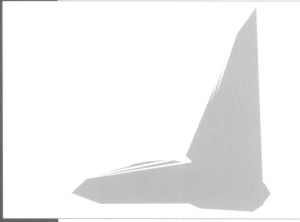

1. We're going to draw a quick and simple background. In the first place, we should prepare a base color for the general tone of the image. We'll give it this shape on account of the composition.

2. We should use perspective to differentiate the floor from the sides.

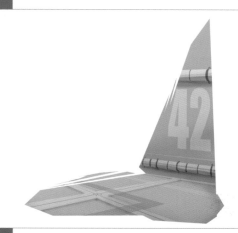

3. The next step is to shape the background elements, such as the piping and metallic plates on the floor. We'll also mark the direction of the lighting, which should be the same as that of the armor.

4. Finally, we'll add the texture of the floor and side. We should look for references to help us draw them. We'll finish by adjusting the scene's lighting.

Finishing Touches

We've added lots of details as final touches to embellish our drawing. We've painted the black line with the color of the visor so it will look more transparent. We've also added airbrushing effects on the areas of light, as well as superimposed text on the armor and weapon to give them more character. The shadow on the floor integrates the figure with its background.

FUTURISTIC

SD Monster Duel

Tokusatsu is a Japanese television genre consisting of action series featuring fantastic heroes and monsters. Within this genre we can find various sub-genres such as *kaiju*, which features gigantic monsters, the most famous of which is *Godzilla*. There's also *kyodai hero*, where gigantic fantastic heroes face the terrible destructive powers of monsters. You could say *Ultraman* is the most famous example of this genre. A third sub-genre is *henshin heroes* where groups of youngsters fight against evil, and receive special powers via a fantastic transformation. Series like *Kamen Rider*, *Kikaider* and *Super Sentai* are prime examples of this genre.

We've decided to adapt a SD style for our illustration. This way we'll be using humor to parody the battle between good and evil, represented by a radioactive reptile monster and the hero who is out to save the city from total destruction.

Shape

Whenever we draw two figures touching each other it's a good idea to begin with the ground they'll be standing on. Afterwards we'll shape the areas where their two bodies meet. Only after having done this can we continue in adapting the rest of the elements to the position we've sketched. In this case we'll be working with *superdeformed* proportions.

Volume

Whenever we want to make something look enormous we should draw it from a low-angle point of view. This way even if we're dealing with tiny figures they'll look like they are gigantic. We'll be using simple rounded volumes for the monster since its arms and legs are short and funny.

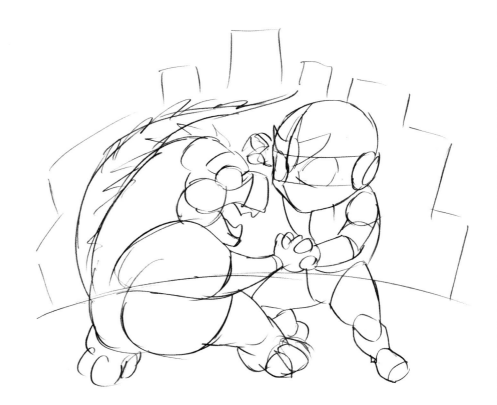

Anatomy

We have two characters; one is a humanoid wearing a fantastic tight suit, the other is a gigantic monster that looks like a reptile. In this section we'll focus on the monster, using a few different tricks to give him a fierce look. We'll give him enormous fangs, sharp scales, a crest on his back, claws and a ferocious threatening look. A monster like this, with SD proportions can look quite funny.

Final Sketch

Once we've defined our monster we'll move on to the hero of the illustration, which we'll be fitting with a tight suit. His helmet is the most important element here. We can give him elements that bring to mind famous genre films and series from the 70's, such as enormous glasses. Next we'll complete the background we began sketching in the previous steps. We'll finish the illustration by adding some more monsters with a simple city to serve as a background.

Lighting

In this kind of drawing it's important to be concise and to learn to simplify shapes. The same thing happens when we're drawing shadows. It's important to define each volume in a simple and direct way. The best thing is to stick to the volumes used when shaping in order to highlight the characters properly. We'll differentiate the background from our main characters by giving it a flatter dimension, in other words, one without shadows.

Flat Colors

It's necessary to radically separate the background from the main characters. We'll resort to a few different tactics to accomplish this. First of all, we'll give the background a neutral color, and fill the foreground with bright, flashy colors. We'll use green for the reptile, and a more extreme combination of red and white for our hero's clothes.

Shading

Let's pay attention to the different textures and effects. Looking at his helmet we see a band that is darker in color, dividing light and shaded tones, proof that the material is shinier than his clothes, where the tones evolve in a simpler manner. We can also see sharp contrast on his glasses thanks to the white area reflecting a gleam of light.

Tips and Tricks

1. Rather than use black, paint their outlines with darker, more saturated tones from the same chromatic spectrum.

2. Another way of breaking down colors without blurring them is to mix successive color tones as in the example.

3. The composition's background centers the image, creating a circular effect. This way we get viewers to fix their attention on the center of action.

Finishing Touches

By following these steps we'll achieve our objective. By painting the lines of background elements with less saturated colors and without drawing their shadows, we create a false effect of aerial perspective that successfully separates the foreground from the background. The final layer, in the shape of a semi-circle, contrasts with the buildings in tone and color, thus creating a third plane behind all the elements.

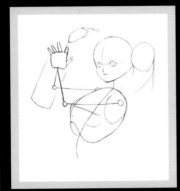

Bionic Girl

One of the most exploited combinations we can find in *manga* is beauty and sweetness contrasted with brute force, and bionic beings have clearly set the standard in this area. Lots of stories have been cut from this cloth. *Gumn*, for example, is about a war robot with an angelic and childlike appearance, while *Saber Marionette J* tells us about the adventures of a group of robot dolls with enormous force but juvenile personalities. Another example, although more focused towards the character's human nature is *Video Girl Ai* by Masakazu Katsura. In short, bionic beings are characters created to entertain every type of reader and ones which fall somewhere between human beings and those of clearly synthetic origin. Whether in epic tales or in the course of daily affairs, *mangas* featuring these characters are among the biggest hits of the genre, with some of them even being best-sellers in their native country.

Shape

We want to show great detail when defining our figure's main characteristics, so we've chosen a close-up of her face and trunk in order to give greater detail to formal elements such as her facial expressions. Arch the back far enough to create an adequate counterweight to the mechanical arm. Use undefined lines to mark the area where the main volumes will be located.

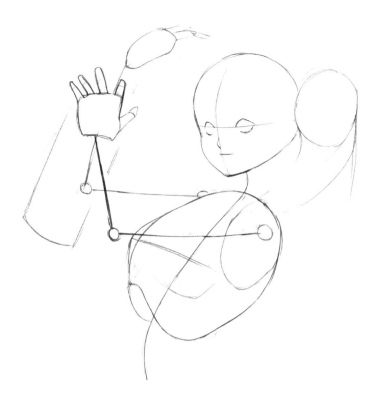

Volume

Let's begin to draw the character's face, bearing in mind that this will be one of the drawing's key elements. In the same way, define the volumes of the various parts of the mechanical arm and its articulations. Add the volume of her hair, especially the pigtail closest to the viewer and the lock of hair that comes out on top of the headphones.

Anatomy

Maintain the rigidity of the volume lines by marking the metallic elements: we should also make the skin that's visible look a bit more elastic. The mechanical arm's hand should show tension. We'll give her face a placid look with large, well-defined eyes. Later on, when we work with colors, we'll finish defining the kind of personality we're looking to create.

Final Sketch

Finish drawing the mechanical arm and use it as a reference to define the rest of the accessories in the drawing. Uncover more areas, as if the character were undergoing a check-up: this will give you more spectacular results. Let's also define the background decoration. We'll draw the left half of the cybernetic motif separately, and later we'll use the computer to clone it on the right.

Lighting

A single light source on the left is enough to illuminate the character properly. Since we're dealing with a synthetic being, use bright highlights on her skin and hair to give her that 'non-human' look that is characteristic of bionic beings. Chrome areas should be done by playing with a range of dark tones in order to create strong contrasts.

Flat Colors

It's a good idea to use pastel colors as a base. We can leave the main shadows of the skin more or less unshaped for now. Later we'll build her anatomy in a more elaborate manner. We'll use less contrast on the part that surrounds the figure. The idea is to make sure the decorative motif doesn't swallow our figure and take attention away from it.

1. Use shading to shape her hairstyle.

2. Use fading to add volume. Now add the highlights.

3. Finish her hair with darker shadow tones and bright highlights.

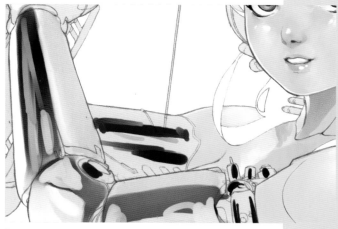

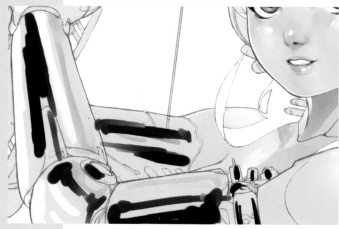

1. Create patches of color that follow the direction and volume of the metallic areas.

2. Shape the patches of colors forming the base of the chromatic area with the fade tool. Add light nuances.

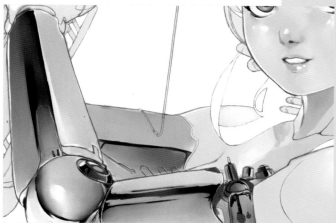

3. Repeat the previous step, but now add shadows to the chrome area.

4. Fade and add even more shades on the plates covering the ribs.

Shading

Use the same procedure as we used in *Combat Armor* when painting the mechanical arm, but without putting too much emphasis on the chrome areas. Repeat the process with the outline of the mechanical decoration. The skin must also look tangible. Using white on the highlights of the flesh will make her look like a doll.

1. Actually this step would be placed before the "Shading" section. It's the first base for patches of color.

2. Use fading when working with shaded tones to shape the chrome of the headphones.

3. We'll add white lines to the contour lines of some of the pieces, thus giving them more volume.

Finishing Touches

Add patches of colors and imperfections to visually age the decoration, making it more matt and devoid of the intensity of the chrome areas. We don't want the metallic parts to look like they just came out of a factory. Use the fine airbrush on some of the brighter lights of the metallic pieces. Lastly, give the character some more personality by adding some decorative motifs.

Space Adventurer

Anti-heroes or scoundrels with a knack for always being in the wrong place? In the world of *manga* and *anime*, the role of the space adventurer has always taken from classical literature sources: transferred from pirate tales and from the more stereotypical westerns, in a context of star-covered galaxies. The genre reached its apex during the late 70's and early 80's on the heels of the success of the first *Star Wars* trilogy. The space adventurer is always surrounded by characteristic elements, such as his spaceship and loads of special weapons. The pillars of this genre are to be found in the work of Leiji Matsumoto and his tortured *Capitan Harlock*, who navigates through space in his *Arcadia* spaceship with the mysterious passenger 42. Another good example is the charismatic and womanizing *Space Adventure Cobra* by Buichi Terasawa, who has a synthetic arm hiding his *psychogun*. More recent works such as *Cowboy Bepop* and *Outlaw Star* have followed in the footsteps of the classics and kept the genre alive.

Shape

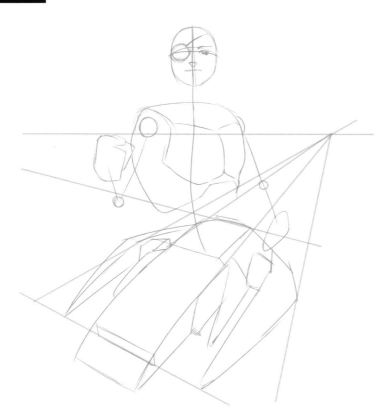

Using Buichi Terasaw's *Cobra* as a reference, we've created a classical composition similar to that of a movie billboard from the 80's, with the hero in the center. We'll set the scene placing an imaginary horizon over which we'll draw the base of the spaceship. We can use a perspective with two vanishing points in order to give more volume. Put the character in an arrogant pose. Lightly sketch his facial features.

Volume

At this stage we'll define the volume of the spaceship and erase the reference lines of the previous steps. We'll use volume to give our hero an athletic build that matches the character we're trying to give him. Look for shapes that aren't too exaggerated and define the hand in the foreground, as well as his foreshortened arm, with simple geometric figures.

Anatomy

To capture the character's pulp-like nature, we'll give his facial features a realistic treatment, with a defiant expression that seems to be teasing as well. Highlight his athletic nature by defining the muscles that will be more or less visible in the final drawing. Try to use his pose to reflect confidence as well as a state of comfort. Remember that this character has to come across as being a real big-shot.

Final Sketch

Finish drawing the character in a simple manner, without overloading his clothing. A tight short-sleeved shirt and vest is all he needs. Try to keep the drawing clean. We'll use color to work the wrinkles. Add characteristic elements such as his futuristic eye-patch and gun. Gather references when drawing your own spaceships. We've taken the dynamic shape of a Formula 1 racecar to draw our main spaceship.

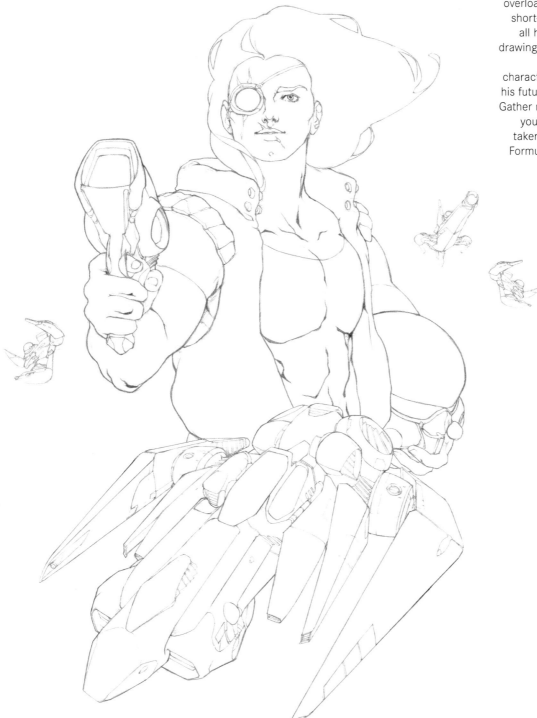

Lighting

We'll use a version of our final sketch done in shades of gray so we can see exactly how lighting is going to work in this illustration. There are three main light sources. The first will be the beam of light from the spaceship itself, which falls on his helmet and vest. The second is the supernova behind our character, which illuminates his face and the enemy spaceships. And finally, there's an independent light which will serve to give the character contrast.

Flat Colors

Tone the illustration with a range of tones that go from less bright (for background elements) to increasingly bright elements (for the main spaceship). This will help you separate planes and create depth when it comes to the time for painting your illustrations. We can add more emphasis by coloring main elements with bright, lively colors, such as red or orange.

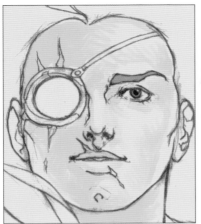

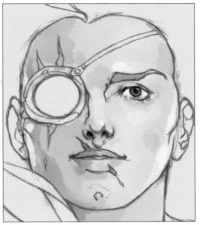

1. Create an initial color base, paying attention to the two light sources that affect the adventurer's face.

2. Use the background colors to cover the left part of his face, and white on the right side. This will help us differentiate where the lights come from better, and give the drawing a greater dimension.

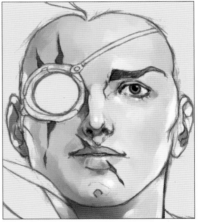

3. Use the fade tool on your program of choice to create the color volumes.

4. Add a third tone of shading to enrich the drawing. Use it to define his main facial features.

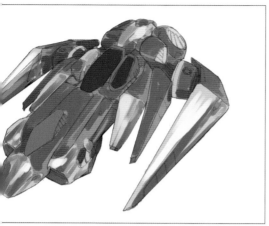

Use more dynamic lines to create the base for metallic areas.

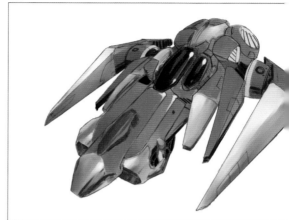

2. The light coming from the spaceship itself marks strong contrasts. Begin to mark the main shadows.

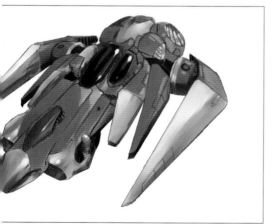

Add more light and shadow.

4. Lastly, go over the outlines of the main pieces to give them more volume and contrast with their shadows even more.

Shading

At this stage we've almost finished the illustration. Add highlights to some of the seams of the jacket which contrast with its dark color. This will reinforce the notion that it's a plastic material. We'll define the background with two patches of two different colors that complement each other well. Use the airbrush to create splashes that will form a starry horizon.

1. Use cold colors to paint enemy spaceships. Keep the atmosphere light on this account.

2. A heavy shadow on the opposite side of the light source will help create more contrast and volume.

3. Define the lights with more visible shapes and clean up the contour lines.

4. Digital color enables us to use a number of tricks, especially come time for playing with logotypes.

5. The layer system allows us to paint an element such as this logo on top of the base color, in this case the shirt. Adapt the logo to the wrinkles of the shirt and shade using the color of the shirt but use a darker hue.

Finishing Touches

We'll add the hero's symbol to his spaceship and enrich the illustration with lots of effects. Paint the gun the same way we did the background, and add highlights on each of the spaceships. This will be enough to give all areas of the drawing movement. We can finish by drawing white contours around the character to make him stand out even more as the central element of our illustration.

Cybercop

In a not too distant future where urban guerillas rule the streets of the main megalopolises, the police force is a shadow of what it used to be. Only this cybercop is capable of deterring and frightening away delinquents. This stereotype, which has often been exploited in cinema and comics, is indebted to the world of *manga*. Cybercops are the subject of lots of *mangas*, which contain a sociological background related to the fear of overcrowding and overpopulation, and doubts as to how humanity will solve these kinds of problems in a not too distant future. While questions like these were pondered in works like *Patlabor* and *Appleseed* giving the machine a secondary role, in others like *Eight Man*, this figure was treated as a superhero. Whatever the case, this half-man/half-machine and 100% policeman will certainly never go out of fashion.

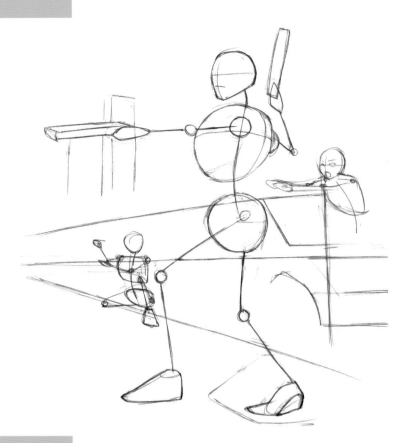

Shape

We'll sketch a complete scene, a shootout, where the more elements we add the better. Mark a horizon and use it as a reference. Give the character a determined pose, with certain rigidity: it's important to show his mechanical origin. We'll use less tense lines for the other characters. Let's arch the back of the policewoman forwards.

Volume

Sketch all the background elements in their basic shapes. It's important to outline the main figures in this step. Let's draw the cybercop with robust volumes and lightly define his armor. Go over the contours, especially those of the guns, to separate them from the background. Create the volumes of the buildings we'll be using as a reference for constructing the background later on.

Anatomy

In this exercise, anatomy is not a fundamental concern, but it will help us understand proportions better and the position of some elements. In this case, foreshortening his front foot and creating tension in his shoulders can be used to build on armor afterwards. Define the cybercop's hair and facial features. The tension in his arms and the movement of his hair help make him look more believable.

Final Sketch

We'll complete the drawing by detailing the armor as much as possible. Use common sense when drawing this kind of illustration. Knee and shin guards are reinforced and more resistant, just as the area of the spinal column and head which contrast with the rib chassis or his half-uncovered face. Strive for balance between the beautiful and the practical. Use compact, but dynamic, shapes for the vehicles.

Lighting

The evening light mixes with the light of the explosions we see in the scene. Let's not complicate things too much: we'll give our cybercop armor with chrome elements, but we won't abuse them either. This will save us a lot of work. On the other hand, we must pay attention to where the lights are coming from and the bursts of flame in the car windows.

Flat Colors

Use a flat color to paint the main characters and the body of the vehicles. Use bright, light colors for the cybercop, even in the dark areas of the armor. This way it will stand out against the rest of this baroque scene. Dot the sidewalk with chips and cracks, and in the same manner draw the explosion clouds and the smoke trailing behind our character.

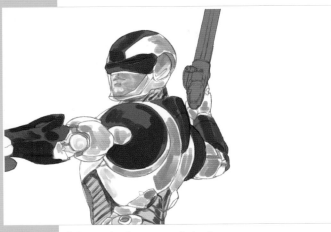

1. Draw the first tone of shading.

2. Fade, shape, add light and another tone of shading.

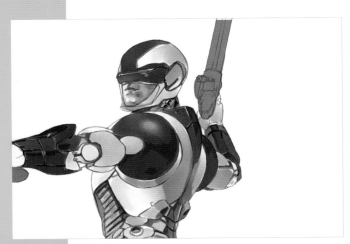

3. Repeat the previous step for the darker parts of the armor.

4. Use shading to finish defining the character's face.

1. Use patches of color to suggest the interior of the vehicle.

2. Contrast the body of the vehicle with white patches of direct light and shadows.

3. Shape the patches of color in the previous step and add some lighter tones to the vehicle's body.

Shading

We've defined the scene pretty well already. On one side we have the sidewalk and the characters on it; on the other side we have the background decoration, which is just about ready to be defined. Now we just have to add some effects, like muddying the various elements of the illustration with splashes of color and texture.

Tips and Tricks

1. This step will help you create a simple, but effective, bullet hole.

2. Now it's time for the bullet hole.

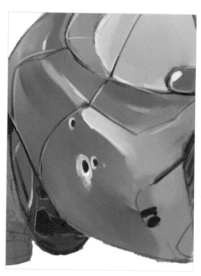

3. Lastly, we'll use the fading tool so that it doesn't just look like a patch of color anymore.

Finishing Touches

We've finished the illustration by adding a blue sky that will make the reflections on the cybercop more coherent. On the other hand, we've also gone and given the floor different textures until it resembles asphalt, and added some splashes of color to create a sense of movement.

409

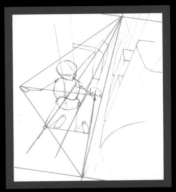

Bounty Hunter

The cyberpunk style which was in vogue in the mid 80's thanks in part to films like *Blade Runner* and novels written by writers such as William Gibson, Bruce Sterling and Rudy Rucker, also became a common mode of expression in science fiction *manga*. Authors such as Otomo and Asamiya would go on to construct worlds of impossible, post-apocalyptic cities where high technology contrasted with the barbarity ruling the streets. Our character, the bounty hunter, is set in these surroundings. In this case we'll be drawing a beautiful woman loaded with a whole lot of weapons, a very popular icon closely connected with the world of *manga*. Shirow, with *Dominion* and *Ghost In the Shell*, and closer to the MTV style, Kenichi Sonoda and his designs for *Bubble Gum Crisis*, are good examples of this tendency. Another relevant work that also shares this theme is *Gumn*, also known as *Battle Angel Alita*.

Shape

This time we're going to make things difficult for ourselves by drawing a setting that will be rather complex. The bounty hunter is on a cornice from which we can see part of a busy avenue. Try not to lose track of the perspective. Use two points for it: the nearer of the two will help you position the height of the buildings, and the further one will mark depth.

Volume

Mark the basic shapes of the main buildings to differentiate them from each other so they don't just look like they all form part of the same volume. As far as the character is concerned, define the various parts of her special outfit and trace the *jetpack* or on-board computer. Remember that this kind of equipment is integral to the character, so don't skimp on detail.

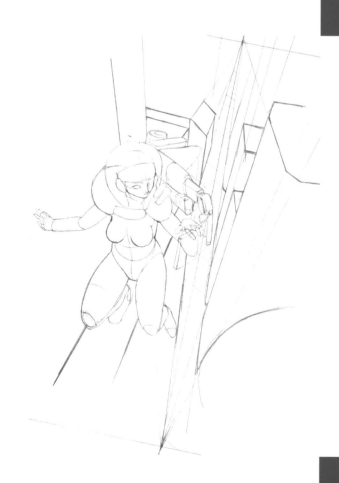

Anatomy

Take a good look at the pronounced effect the high-angle perspective has on the character. Pay special attention when foreshortening the leg that is closer to us and the arm touching the tactile screen. The pose must be calm; the Bounty Hunter is used to this kind of situation. Add an intermediate stage in the background to understand the transition to the final sketch and the construction of the buildings.

Final Sketch

Completely define the elements of her outfit. When finishing the *jetpack* keep its functionality in mind. It's quite big, but it has to look light in order for her to carry it more or less comfortably. We'll adjust her hairstyle and studded shoulder-pads to the cyberpunk style. The outfit must fit like a glove, but using plates to separate some of the parts will help make it look harder.

Lighting

The illustration is conditioned by the light coming from the main street, but the *jetpack* tactile screen and the tallest buildings that are nearest our character will help us tone the illustration. Despite this, bear in mind that the light will go from being less intense in the foreground, to being brighter on the sidewalk, apart from the reflection on her suit.

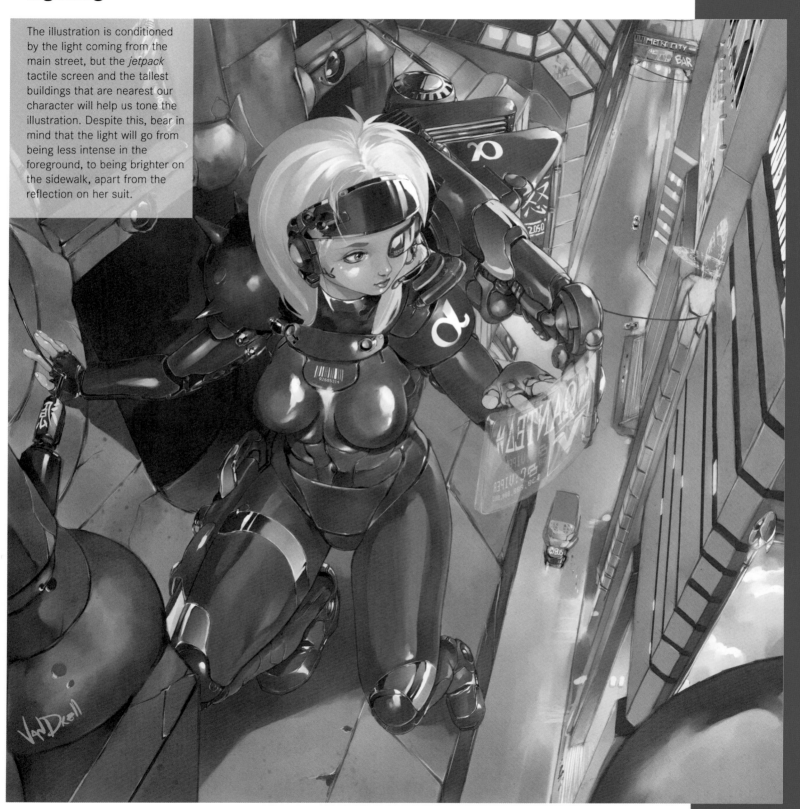

Flat Colors

We'll draw our character using an off-tone as a base that contrasts with her skin and hair colors. Begin by using the base color to paint the background, and then go about shaping the elements little by little. Use dark patches of color for the objects in the foreground and begin adding light tones that aren't too bright on some of the buildings and the street.

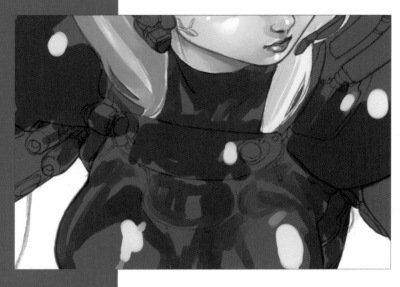

Tips and Tricks

1. We'll add shadows to her outfit, even though it is already quite dark. We'll also mark points of light on the smoothest surface areas.

2. After shaping the character's anatomy we'll go over the darker areas with another tone of shading.

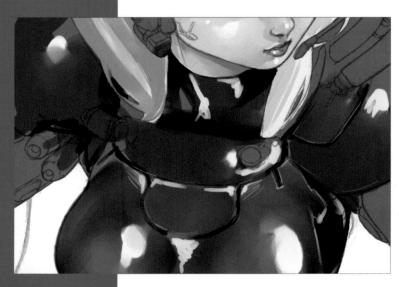

3. Use the tone of the tactile screen to illuminate the rest of her outfit.

Tips and Tricks

1. Use fading to create the volumes of the cornice. Begin adding imperfections.

2. Repeat the previous step, using shading to go over the imperfections.

3. Paint lines of light over the blocks and cracks of the cornice.

Shading

Now our background is more or less defined. However, we still have to add lots of nuances, in lighting as well as in shading. Let's use intermediate tones for this. The outfit is already finished, but the closer it is to the *jetpack's* screen, the greener it will be. On the other hand, look at how her lens is affected by the ambient light and the green tone emanating from it. This transition of colors makes the materials we paint look more realistic.

1. Finish doing the details of the street and the buildings. Look how we can use patches of color to create the effect of an interior in the distance.

2. Digital coloring allows us to adapt other drawings to decorate streets with billboards. This is an example of a color sketch being reused to serve as a billboard.

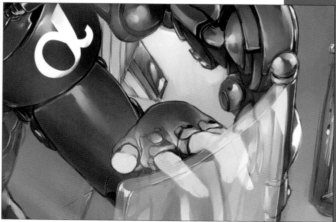

3. Play with the eraser's opacity and intensity when creating transparencies.

4. Add highlights with the fine airbrush.

5. Repeat the first step for typographies.

Finishing Touches

Go over the lights of the buildings surrounding our bounty hunter by using the fine airbrush, an essential tool for achieving more realistic drawings. Finish with whatever typographic elements you feel are necessary for making the illustration look more realistic. Now you can say your work is finished.

Power Rangers

Power Rangers is a United States television series based on the *Tokusatsu Super Sentai* series, a Japanese television science-fiction genre. Likewise, it's also the name used in the West for this variant on the prolific Japanese genre better known as *sentai*. Although within this subgenre we can find different types of characters, such as *Ultraman* or *Masked Rider*, the most famous in the United States is what we see here, one which was a television hit for numerous years. It depicts a group of youngsters chosen to defend world peace, wearing colorful suits and controlling giant toy robots. This idea has been exploited in countless *animes* which combine everyday affairs with repetitive fight situations against the bad guy of the moment. Among *mangakas* the best examples outside of this action series would probably be *Comando G*, *Dai Apolon* and *Saber Rider*.

Shape

The main idea for this illustration is a core composition showing the protagonists of the story backed by their vehicles. Position the horizon over which we'll construct the base of the vehicles. This will visually compensate the depth established by the characters. Lightly sketch the main character's vehicle and the robot in the back.

Volume

Begin defining the shapes of the vehicles and sketch their animal features. The good thing about aerial space is that there isn't a clear horizon line, which allows us to combine different vanishing points for different objects. Draw the characters so they are solid, making sure they don't fall. Give some of them some light movement so they don't look too rigid.

Anatomy

Give the rangers an athletic
look. Since part of their
anatomy will be visible in the
end on account of their tight
outfits, don't overuse the lines.
Pay special attention when
finishing characters whose
faces will be left uncovered.
Bear in mind how the slightly
low-angle view will affect
perspective as we define the
characters in a more or less
realistic style.

Final Sketch

Each vehicle has its own function, besides being a series of elements where each is different from the next. Look for combinations that match their pilot's character or, in this case, the animal they represent: the snake with its amphibian chassis, the tiger with its all-terrain claws, etc. Design the helmets in the same fashion, so they can be identified with their vehicles. Lastly, draw the wrinkles in their boots and gloves.

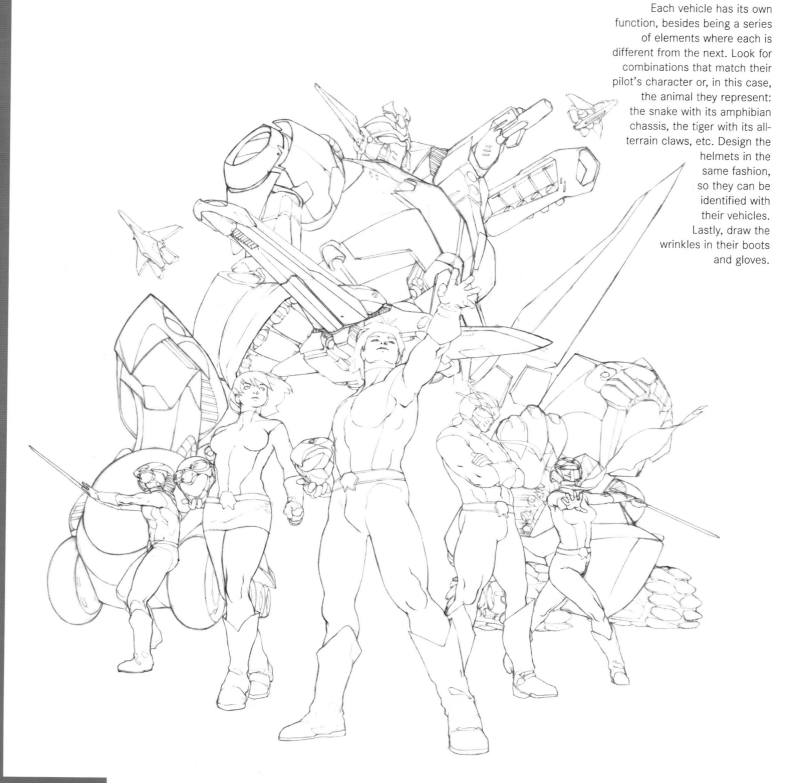

Lighting

The best way of transmitting the naive spirit of this kind of series is to use bright colors and resort to spectacular visual elements, such as explosions and fire. For this we'll use a daylight ambience and a second, more intense, light source that comes from some kind of explosion located behind the characters.

VanDrell

Flat Colors

Lightly color the pavement to position the characters better, and begin defining the explosion and the clouds in the sky. Use bright colors, but save white for finishes. Paint the base of the vehicles and characters differentiating the various parts that make them up. This can help us later as we paint each individual element without having to do new layers.

Tips and Tricks

1. Create a base of hues with light and shade in each of the robot's elements.

2. Solid volumes are created when we fade. Use light colors for lighting.

3. Go over shaded areas.

1. With a single tone of shading, and varying the pressure of your pencil stroke, you can create a chiaroscuro base to work over.

2. We can shape the volumes better by applying the same treatment with the fade tool.

3. This step-by-step method will also help us when it comes to painting the vehicles. Add shadows over the tonal base of the previous detail.

4. Take a general look at the drawing and finish adding any shadows that are needed. Retouch those which don't look realistic.

5. You can also add highlights and reflections while following the instructions in the previous step.

Shading

The colors the characters wear must differentiate them, since the explosion and daylight will make the objects project intense shadows over them. Mark definitive shadows on the pavement. Think about how the explosion will affect the metal parts of the vehicles and how the chrome areas reflect off each other.

1. We have the Ikari Studio logotype on a separate layer.

2. We can use the "distort" option to adapt it to the shape of the shoulder and eliminate excesses.

3. We'll degrade the logotype so it blends in better.

Finishing Touches

Let's finish by defining the background and floor, giving them some finishing touches. The final step will be to add the trail behind the main vehicle, light splashes of color and logotypes for each of the characters. Now you can run a survey on your friends to find out which is their favorite in the group.

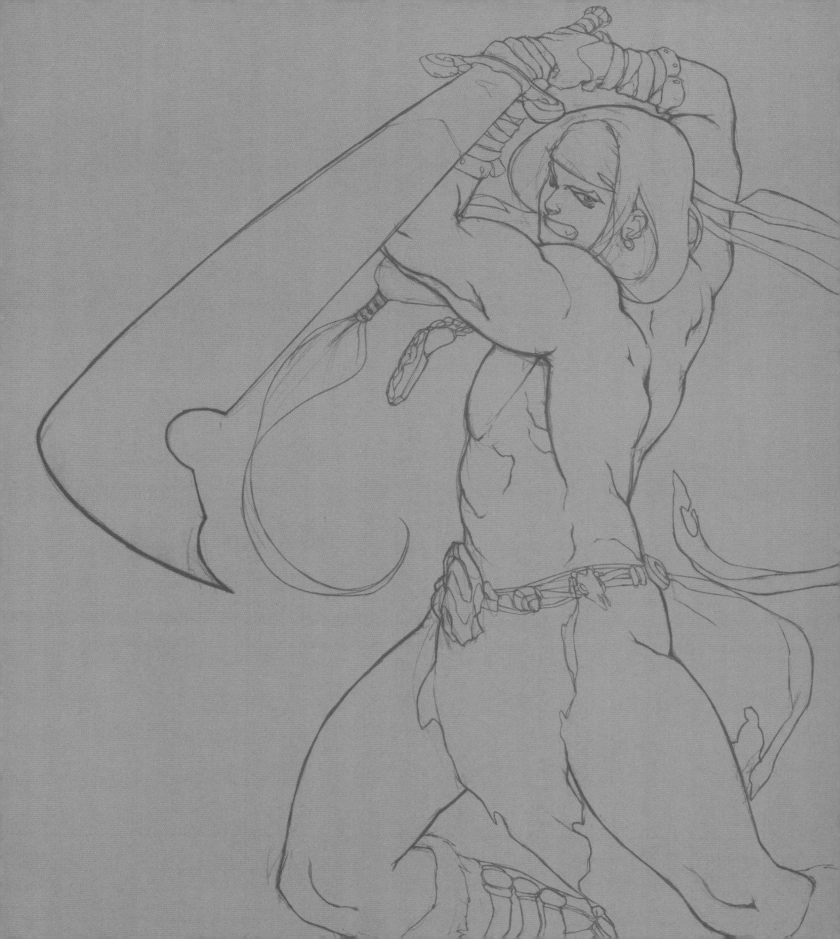

HEROIC FANTASY

SD Swordmaster

Barbarian

Butcher

Sorceress

SD Swordmaster

Throughout the whole book we have seen various examples of *superdeformed* characters, depicted in a style which spares no one in its humor, while still pertaining to the fantasy genre. In fact, fantasy is definitely the genre with far and away more SD parodies than any other. For the most part, the explanation for their popularity lies in the fact that the origin of many of these fantasy stories can be found in the world of role-playing games. In Japan, these games are closely connected to the world of video-games. We can easily find hundreds of fantasy video-games in any Japanese shopping mall or specialized store. As far as the legendary works of the genre are concerned, we can't miss mentioning the animated parodies of the *Record of Lodoss War* series, made in the short-film format and very popular with fans, and also versions of classic role-playing games such as Falcom's *Y's*.

Shape

The stereotype of a knight with pets such as fairies and goblins serves as the basis of this illustration. So we'll use a composition that integrates these characters. The knight must show movement as if coming towards the reader. Despite the small proportions, be careful when foreshortening his arm and legs. Define the basic shapes of his face, since this is an important part of the drawing.

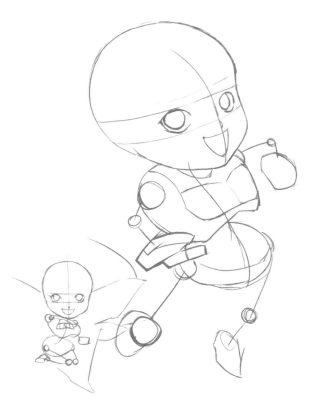

Volume

Sketch the main parts of his armor, such as the shoulder pads and, especially his sword. Locate and begin drawing bits of the characters' hair, keeping movement in mind. Do the fairy's wings, in order to successfully compose the composition. Sketch the characters' expressions and mouths, but still leave them uncompleted.

Anatomy

Finish defining the two characters' faces. Also use clear and clean lines to perfectly define the lines of their eyes. The knight's anatomy guides us in understanding how to foreshorten his arm better. Just as when drawing his face, use round shapes and make sure you don't overload the image with unnecessary lines so that we keep the stocky style we're looking for.

Final Sketch

Play around with the movement of the knight's cape and the leaf the fairy is on top of, fitting them into the general composition. When drawing armor, draw details but don't overload them too much. Remember that SD drawings often stand out for their apparent simplicity. Give the illustration greater depth by using a line hierarchy that makes the protagonist's hand and sword wider.

Lighting

In this illustration we have two different light sources. On the one hand we have the ambient light that comes from behind our characters, and on the other hand, we also have a frontal light source. The highlights on the hero's clothes and armor must be very pronounced and marked so they almost look like satin.

Flat Colors

Both characters should be painted with different, but matching, colors. We'll tone down the colors of our protagonist in order to place him physically behind the fairy. This way we'll be giving our image greater depth. Let's use a range of brighter, more autumnal colors for our fairy.

Tips and Tricks

1. Even though we're going to give it a more pictorial finish, it's still an SD drawing. We'll shape the hair using large patches of shadow and different shades on his bangs.

2. The volumes we've created are simple, but they perfectly describe the shape of his hair. Add light the way you would in an *anime*-style drawing.

3. Repeat the previous steps while following the shape of his face. Now add lighting details. Go over the lines of his eyes as if you were inking the drawing, giving him a more powerful gaze.

Tips and Tricks

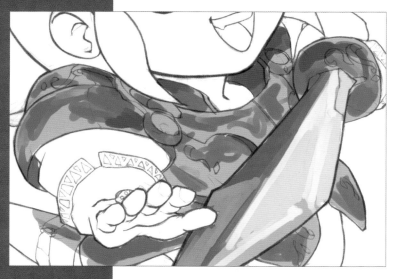

1. When painting armor, it's very important to look at the way the light falls. In this case the light source on the left creates a series of shadows on the armor and especially on his sword.

2. Use the fade tool to construct his armor. Now separate the decoration on it with shinier tones. Add more shades to the rest of the elements.

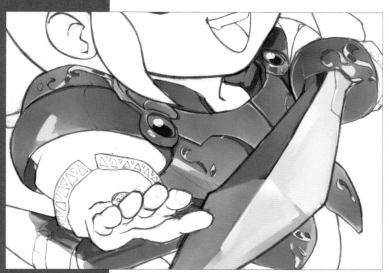

3. Finally add lights and shadows.

Shading

Follow the same process when it's time to paint the fairy. Make sure the colors of the wing and hair look lively enough, and that they achieve the depth we're trying to create. We can convey greater movement if we use fading on the pompoms of her hair as if it were a comb. With the characters' colors almost finished, we only need to add a background that balances our composition.

1. We'll use colors that aren't too saturated and repeat the procedure by going from greater to lesser intensity in creating planes of different depth.

2. Perform an initial shaping of all the elements and then add tones of shading.

3. Repeat step 2, giving greater detail to those elements that are nearest.

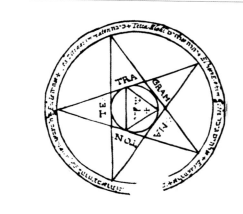

4. The final job doesn't have to be excessively elaborated. The end-effect should be casual and youthful.
Lastly, let's add a magical motif that helps us separate the characters even more and highlights the way we've played with different planes.

Finishing Touches

Here we can see our finished illustration. All that's left is to powder some light dots behind the fairy. This is a trick that helps bring the character closer to the reader, just as putting elements behind a character would in any other drawing. This gives the illustration depth, making it a 3D illustration.

Barbarian

The adventures and misfortunes of this classic and arrogant character with his own peculiar code of ethics, have monopolized the vignettes of some of the famous *mangas*. Stories featuring barbarians usually take place in settings devastated by evil forces where the weak don't have anything to put in their mouths. This environment is home to an atypical hero who prefers to look for a good fight before he thinks about concepts like goodness or justice. Although the *Conan* barbarian archetype was established by the American writer Robert E. Howard in 1932, we can also find examples of heroic fantasy in Japan. The tireless Hagaiwara, for example, gave us a wild, and at the same time, fun glimpse of the sword and sorcery genre in his *manga Bastard* where the minimalist philosophy of the barbarian universe was reflected in a clear and direct way: shoot first. Ask questions later. Just in case.

Shape

Barbarians usually have their own special methods of attacks with which to fight epic battles. We'll try to capture this moment in our drawing. In order to put emphasis on the violence of this barbarian attack, choose a pose with lots of movement. Take a look at the arrows that indicate the exaggerated twisting of his body. Arch his back to go along with the movement. Lastly, define the position of the sword.

Volume

Thanks to the volumes you can get a better understanding of his torso's movement. Define the hero's muscles making sure you keep as much of the figure's gestures as possible. Avoid drawing rigid volumes. The character should look like he's moving and display maximum flexibility. Lightly sketch the hard features of his face.

Anatomy

Define the main muscle groups of his arms and back, since these are a primary element in the drawing. Finish his facial expression: it has to convey the effort and fury behind his attack. This character has a lot of personality. Beginning with a sketch of the sword's handle, we'll define the two hands with their fists almost clenched. His entire anatomy must show toughness, strength and tension.

Final Sketch

In this case this step is merely a formality, although we can use it to give the attack more movement. The loincloth and the ribbon in his hair will be drawn in the opposite direction to where he's jumping, while his hair and the talisman around his neck will hang suspended in the air. We'll give definition to the sword to add more depth, using thicker lines for the areas that are nearest us.

Lighting

In these last two sections we'll be looking at another way of using digital color to get results that look similar to classical illustrations. The first step will be to do away with inking and go straight to color. In our lighting we'll begin using a low saturation version of the final sketch to help give us an idea about the shades of color we'll be using. In this drawing we'll have a dim frontal light source that gets overshadowed by the lighting from the super-attack.

Flat Colors

We'll choose earthy tones for the barbarian's boots and accessories. Although we'll be using a very light color for his clothes, let's use a base other than white in order to achieve an end result of dirtiness. Our barbarian roams across deserts and mountains and faces evil monsters and wizards almost daily, so he doesn't have free time to stop and wash his clothes.

Shading

The shininess of his sword grabs the reader's attention and makes the weapon an integral part of the all-round picture of his super-attack. Define the wrinkles in his clothes using two tones of shading and finish all the outfit's ornamental aspects the same as we did with the sword: going over the contour lines with a light color.

1. We'll paint the character's torso using a combination of two tools: the paintbrush will create a tonal base, and the fade tool will give shape to his muscles. This will be the basic formula for painting the majority of the elements.

2. After the initial base, add shade and a lighter shade of color to the main light points and use patches of white for the light itself.

3. Notice how we shaped the patches of color between the previous step and this one to give them volume.

4. Always finish with the lighter shades of light. Go over the important lines of the drawing as if you were inking it with the shading tone.

Finishing Touches

Another key aspect of our drawing is the correct use of layering to add elements such as typographies, textures and decorative motifs such as those which cover our barbarian's loincloth. Decorative motifs always help give an illustration a more elaborate and realistic finish. Lastly, let's define this super-attack with splashes of color, but take care not to overuse them.

Butcher

Bloodthirsty, merciless, relentless and visually excessive, the butcher plays a similar role in the fantasy genre as the gang member does in the post-apocalyptic genre. He's a brainless enemy, a mass of muscles without principles or compassion, feared by innocent people and manipulated by the wicked. Usually these characters are of disproportionate size, capable of brandishing gigantic weapons and often they have serious deformations. They usually meet their end at the hands of the hero of the day, who generally follows the eye-for-an-eye principle and makes them pay dearly for the injustices and atrocities they've committed. Clear examples can be found in previously mentioned works such as *Bastard*, or in a more childish way, *Dragon Quest*. But where the butcher is really shown at his craziest is in *Berserk* by Kentaro Miura, which depicts possibly the freakiest and most spectacular beasts in the whole of medieval fantasy.

Shape

We should try to capture the moment when this maniac leaves his den in search of prey. To do this, we'll position our character so it looks like he's going to take someone by surprise, as if he were coming straight out of the ground. When shaping him, we should think about his enormous body proportions, especially his torso, shoulders and arms. Arch the line of his back to balance his hammer's counterweight, and begin defining the space he will occupy.

Volume

Since anatomy is the most representative feature of this exercise, we must be very careful when shaping his body. Use more marked volumes for his arms and legs, so they look hard. Begin studying the position of his face and hair. In the same way, position the hammer in the scene and sketch its basic shape.

Anatomy

When we come to define his outstanding muscles, we'll use the references we spoke about in the introduction, since we must make him look wicked and grotesque. Make sure you exaggerate his shoulders and arms, which should have a brutish look. Bear in mind the malleability of his enormous stomach and the creases that form in the areas where his figure flexes. Give his hands and feet a rough and gnarled look.

Final Sketch

His armor must look worn, so let's add some cracks and imperfections to it. Give his mask a fierce look to highlight the character's personality. Use macabre elements, like a small skull, to decorate the string of his loincloth. Draw the hammer following the same steps as we did when drawing his armor. It has to look like our butcher has participated in lots of fights.

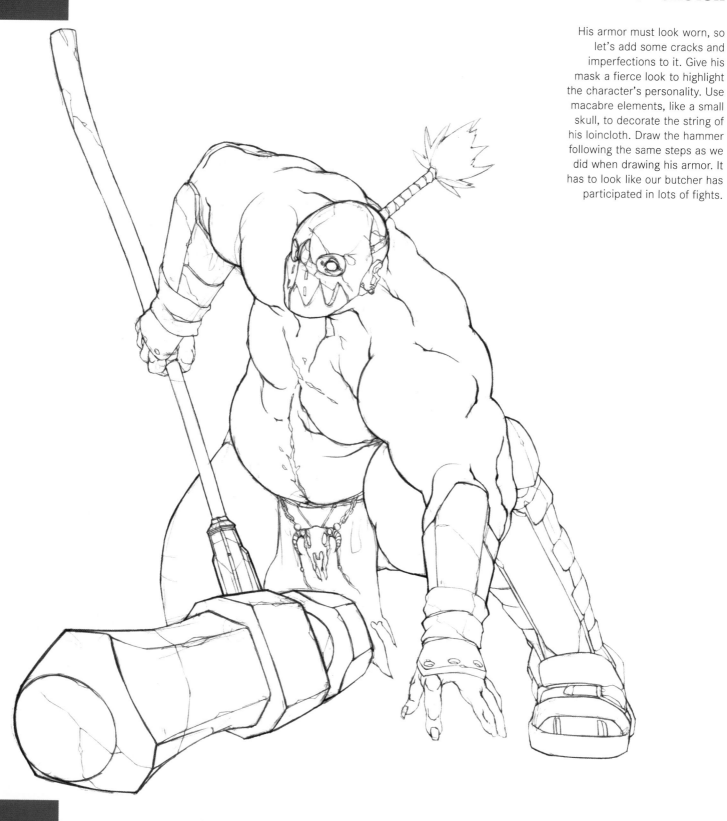

Lighting

A completely frontal light source, without very strong or excessive ambient light, will help us make an illustration which is not very difficult, but still effective and full of impact for the reader. The only area where we will have to make sure we pay special attention is when we study how the light reflects on to the armor's notched metal.

Flat Colors

We'll paint the butcher's armor using colors with a dark base. These colors will also help us use shading to shape the general volumes of different elements of the illustration. We'll use an intermediate color for his skin. As we'll see in the next section, we can make him look quite sickly by using a lighter tone than the one we would use for a normal person's skin.

Shading

Before painting this brute, think about his lifestyle. Confined in places with barely any light, he only sees the sun when he's out fighting. We'll paint his skin a pale, almost ghastly color, without using the lightest tones so we preserve the grimy film that covers him. His armor, worn and filthy, shouldn't have any chrome showing on it. Give it scratches, dents and dry blood stains so it looks more realistic.

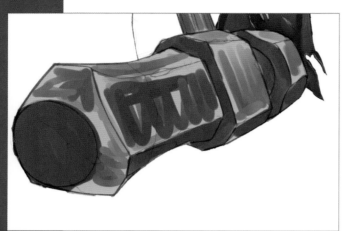

1. Use a tone of shading to create a base.

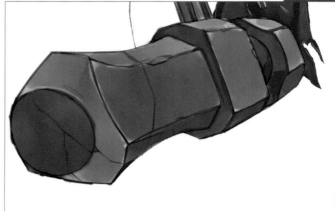

2. Fade the patches of color. Adapt them for each part of the hammer. Put the first red blotches on its point.

3. Use a lighter tone for lighting. We won't be overusing the highlights since it's a stone hammer.

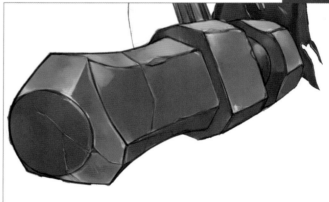

4. Repeat step two. Follow this step-by-step when painting the metal pieces, but add more shades of light and reflection. Remember his armor is supposed to look worn.

Finishing Touches

Use brushstrokes imitating stains and splashes to make his armor and hammer look more battered. Put some magic symbols on his enormous body as if they were tattoos. When painting the ground, follow the same steps as for the hammer, but begin with lighter tones, so that there is greater contrast with the hole our character is coming out of.

Sorceress

In the *Sword and sorcery* genre, among which *Conan* is definitely the leading representative, the figure of the woman has traditionally been reduced to the category of an extra, or a mere object to be enjoyed by men. However, in *manga* we can find honorable exceptions to this unwritten genre rule. In Japanese 'sword and sorcery' stories, the character of the witch, or sorcerer, is usually placed in an ambiguous position with respect to the main hero. Perhaps the sorcerer will wind up helping him, but it's also just as possible that the sorcerer will end up leading the hero into a trap. Whether of unusual beauty or of disgusting ugliness, sorcerers are always a basic element in any good story in this genre. *Dragon Quest*, *Record of Lodoss War*, *Slayers*, *Jester* and *Orphen* are just a small sample of the infinite number of works that depend on the presence of this kind of character.

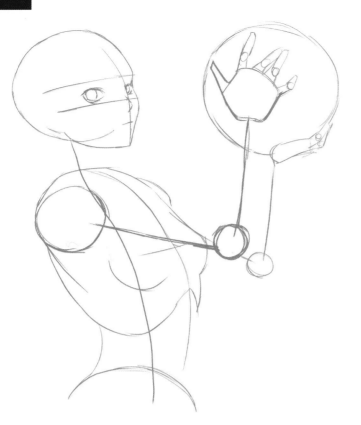

Shape

We'll focus on a plane that's nearer the character, which will help us put greater detail on the element of clothing as well as on her facial features. Position the character holding a glass ball and observing the reader out of the corner of her eye. Arch her back slightly and stiffen the arm holding the sphere, since it's contracted on account of the object's weight.

Volume

Mark the basic shapes of her body, making sure we show basic details of the sorceress' anatomy. Sketch her stern and mysterious expression, since it's the thing that will help give the reader a good idea about the character's personality. Then do the same with a considerable amount of her hair and the crystal ball, which is a very powerful element in itself.

Anatomy

Bearing in mind that her clothing is the most visible and elaborate area of the drawing, the only thing we have to do in this step is finish defining her expression and her hands. Be extremely careful as you outline the look in her eyes and the expression of her lips. When drawing her hands you should highlight the tension in the wrist holding the magical sphere. Lastly, finish drawing her hairstyle.

Final Sketch

Let's now add decorative elements of a magical nature to the character. To differentiate from the "gothic" look, we'll give her a classical look, closer to that of a gypsy. Draw the cloth that's lying over her arm. Focus on the wrinkles that form in the areas where her arm bends, as well as the volumes that form from the way the fabric hangs.

Lighting

A weak zenithal lighting will help us mark the main points of light in the illustration. The main elements are the way light reflects over the crystal ball, the shiny parts of her hair, and how some shadows are projected over the lightest areas of her clothes. When illuminating the ring that surrounds our character, we'll use a frontal light source that highlights its edges as a base.

Flat Colors

We can give our character a more ethnic look by using a palette consisting of shades of brown. The only exception will be the bandana on her head and the thin fabric on her arms, which we'll paint in a dark crimson. Since this is a drawing that requires various stages of color treatment, we'll emphasize the base of some elements, such as her face and shoulder pad. Remember we're dealing with a zenithal light source. Proceed to shape the basic volumes of her face.

Tips and Tricks

1. Fade the base colors. Add shading to the lower eyelid, and some primary lighting.

2. Fade again, this time adding lighter shades for all her face.

3. Define her eyes in the way we've done with SD characters. Use light lines to define her lips and detail her nose.

Tips and Tricks

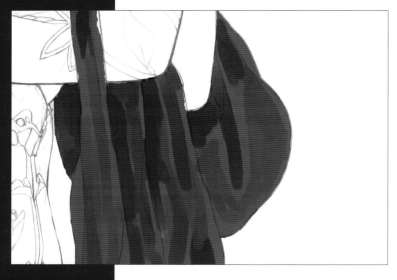

1. Shape the basic wrinkles of the fabrics by following the direction we marked previously with her clothing.

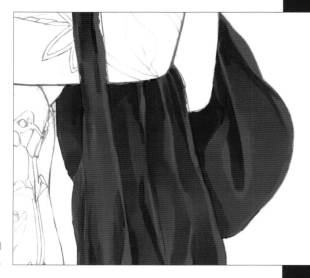

2. Fade the base and add shadows.

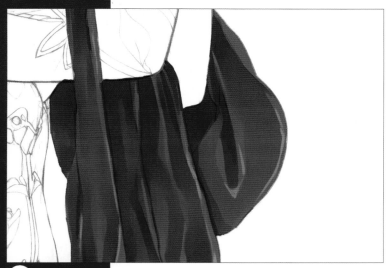

3. Lastly, use a tone of light to finish detailing.

Shading

We'll paint her clothing in dark colors. We'll combine shades of gray on her bodice and darker shadows that will give it a satin look. Her arms and shoulders will have a slightly creamy color. The crystal ball is still in its early stages. We've barely given it a tonal base yet. Since it's a reflective object, make a note of the colors of the objects nearest it.

Tips and Tricks

1. Use the fade tool to give shape to the intermediate patches of color, and add highlighting and shading.

2. Follow the object's spherical shape, and combine its base color with the tones it reflects.

3. Use the fine airbrush and fade tool to define the intense highlights on the crystal ball.

Finishing Touches

The magical symbols and ancient motifs on the cloth and bandana go well with the metallic ring around the illustration. To do this we should create a base on the computer and paint it as if it were a metal object, using splashes of color to emphasize the object's used and worn look. Lastly, the old symbols give it that ancient look which fits in perfectly with the time period we are depicting.

This book was a joint project between Ikari Studio and Estudio Joso. Coordinated by Ikari, a new wave of *manga* illustrators who studied at the Joso School of Comics were given the opportunity to show what good work they're capable of - a similar opportunity to that which Estudio Joso once gave to the members of Ikari Studio.

Ikari would like to thank all the illustrators for their efforts. In addition, we are especially grateful to Estudio Joso for wanting us to continue sharing their dream.

So, to all of you collaborated with us, many, many thanks!